Foreword by Daniel Kobla Glymin

GUARD YOUR *Heart*

KUUKUA MAURICE ANKRAH
VICTORIA TWUM-GYAMRAH

GUARD YOUR HEART

Copyright © KUUKUA MAURICE ANKRAH
VICTORIA TWUM-GYAMRAH, 2024.

All Rights Reserved.

No part of this book may be reproduced in any form by photocopying or by any electronic or mechanical means, including information storage in a retrieval system, without the written permission of both the copyright owner and the publisher of this book.

Unless otherwise stated, all references from the scriptures are quoted from the New King James Bible (2004). Thomas Nelson (Original work published 1982).

ISBN: 978-9988-9394-8-9

Published & Produced By: Kuukua Maurice Ankrah
4C Kwabena Duffuor RD. GL-144-0568

Cover Design By: Eric Nartey.

Edited By: Prince George Sagoe
Layout & Printed By: NSAB Ltd.

For any information on the book or the author, please contact any of the addresses below:

Email: kuukuaankrah@gmail.com
WhatsApp: +233 (0) 27 628 5908

Printed in Ghana.

REVIEWS

I have had an enjoyable time engaging with the book *Guard Your Heart*.

Rarely will you come across a book where the author opens up her life and shares deep and personal stories with you.

This book is truly different!

Its uniqueness lies not only in its simplicity and readability, but it also reveals to us how personal and intimate the fellowship with the Holy Spirit can be and indeed how much the Holy Spirit yearns for it.

In these times when Christians are less concerned about character and conformity with the image of Christ but rather prefer shallow and "quick fix" relationships with the Lord, *Guard Your Heart* refocuses us on the need to walk with the Lord and with one another in love and truth! Indeed, out of the heart are the issues of life, hence the clarion call in this beautiful piece to guard our hearts.

God is looking for clean and purged hearts to pour Himself into and use mightily in this end-time.

This book by Lady Kuukua is so timely, especially in an era where Christian values such as walking in love, forgiveness, long-suffering and self-denial are fast eroding from our Pentecostal and Charismatic circles.

I am of the firm belief that Lady Kuukua is one of such prepared vessels for God's end-time revival agenda. There is an anointing on the book that brings strong conviction.
Be blessed as you read!

- Rev. Felix Agbodeka

A very instructive book, clearly the work of the Holy Spirit. I believe that through this book, the Holy Spirit draws attention to what one needs to do to lead a complete life and attain salvation. It sheds light on the way to become an achieving Christian.

As Christians, it is particularly important to understand, like the sons of Issachar, the times and seasons in which we live, so we can become giants as is prophesied by end-time Christians.

This book, as guided by the Holy Spirit, points the way to purge ourselves of our human weaknesses, thus revitalising our God-created souls, whilst learning obedience and reliance on the Holy Spirit in readiness for the end time exhibition of the power given to Christians. Additionally, the book focuses on lessons that when well-learnt catapult one's relationship with our three-in-one God to unimaginable heights. The writer uses her life experiences to educate readers about the need to invite and rely on the Holy Spirit in every dimension of one's life. In the following paragraphs, I discuss the issues she focuses on that captured my attention:

Praying Answer-Oriented Prayers:
Here she advocates advancing God's Kingdom in prayer and witnessing through testimonies. Matthew 6:33 tells us to work towards advancing God's Kingdom, after which everything we desire shall be provided. God is truthful to His word - He does not change!

A Lesson in Accommodating, Forgiving and Accepting People as They Are:
We mostly complain, focusing on the negative attributes of individuals, forgetting that our God, the Creator, is perfect in that individual. I agree with the need to overcome pride - the harbinger of a person's downfall. The author emphasizes the need to learn to pray with positive intentions for good, God-directed results in all aspects of our lives.

I empathise with her insight into a people prone to condemnation and believe that as a nation, if we adhere to positive directions with the help of the Holy Spirit through fervent prayers, this is certain to propel us and our leaders towards greater societal cohesion. This, the writer time and again shows is a Christian's duty and responsibility. The assurance is that the Holy Spirit gives each Christian the best insight to navigate our lives.

Relationships:

This book puts a lot of emphasis on relationships and the need to pray for our parents, subordinates, employees, and friends. We gain strength from the Holy Spirit to direct our steps in dealing with them. It is a fact that some people are inherently difficult to deal with or love, however, she opines that when we allow the Holy Spirit to take over our thoughts, we gain wisdom and strength to successfully navigate this tricky aspect of human relationships. With the intervention and direction of the Holy Spirit, we shall relate without negative emotions because the Holy Spirit leads and strengthens one to always give detractors the benefit of the doubt.

There are Lessons and Reminders Not to Doubt the Prophet's Word or Direction:

The author enjoins us to believe and have faith in our prophets. She advises that when a man of God gives directions from the "whisperings" of the Holy Spirit, doubting him is tantamount to dishonouring the Holy Spirit - not just the Man of God! This, she says grieves the Holy Spirit. We must be careful not to miss the voice of the Holy Spirit by looking down at the medium He speaks through sometimes.

The Christian and Pride:

The author cautions against this dangerous weakness of Christians who pride themselves in knowing it all. Some put themselves on a pedestal, look down on others - proverbially judge books by their covers, and condemn them. She warns against superiority complexes and the attendant arrogance, which lead some Christians to believe that everyone must recognize and acknowledge them! She opines that it is a wrong attitude that we must all pray to overcome.

Pride our General Weakness:
As the offender or offended, we must as Christians learn to forgive, because forgiveness is in itself a healing balm that soothes the heart. Holding on to hurts and not letting go destroys no one, but one's self.

Our Bodies, the Temple of God; Not A Rubbish Dump:
The author says we are what we eat and should be mindful of treating our bodies as the high seat of God. The Holy Spirit directs us on what to eat. He can even control our cravings. She reminds us to remember that the devil is out to destroy all that God has made beautiful, not only with immorality but with poor unhealthy eating habits.

The writer indirectly is telling all that our diet must be presented to the Holy Spirit for approval and rightly so! She clearly believes the obsession with foods that are unhealthy can only be broken by prayers and faith actions. She clearly states that the Holy Spirit is drawing our attention to aspects of our everyday lives that we must work on as Christians to enjoy breakthroughs in our life journeys.

The gems I have learnt from reading this insightful book are invaluable !!

I wholeheartedly would recommend it to Christians of every level of our study, to emulate our Lord and Saviour. May God, through the Holy Spirit help and lead us all to this all-important realization.

- Ms. Kate Annan Wilberforce

"*Catch us the foxes, The little foxes that spoil the vines, for our vines have tender grapes.*" Song of Solomon 2:15. The seemingly harmless and little (fifteen inches tall) foxes destroy the vines by digging and loosening the soil around them. This action destroys the root system at its most critical and vulnerable stage, severely compromising the very system that ensures the anchorage and nourishment of the tender fruit-laden vines.

Our little foxes are those persistent challenges and besetting sins; the seemingly small, but significant and persistent issues that give the enemy access to the love relationship between us, the bride and Jesus, the Bridegroom.

This, my dear friends, is the crux of my dear sister Kuukua's awesome new book, *Guard Your Heart!*

In her usual relatable and candid (and even sometimes disarmingly unnerving) style, Kuukua pulls no punches as she unreservedly uses her own experiences as case studies to deal with a plethora of 'foxes' that we all can relate to.

From dealing with issues of self-entitlement to ingratitude to simple things like listening to understand, rather than to respond (Stop Fighting Me in Your Head), Kuukua challenges those damaging entrenched attitudes that we all manifest by default; attitudes that we have often imbibed by a training which, for example, teaches us to anticipate and prepare ourselves for all possible outcomes.

The subtle and myriad manifestations of the deadly sin of pride are dealt with in this eye-opening compendium of bite-size topical readings that are each so loaded in themselves!

The new *'Food for Thought'* format adopted in this book is just brilliant because it gives the reader time to ruminate over each key issue being addressed; this essential period of soul searching should, God-willing, culminate in a resolve to repent and embark on a journey that allows for Christ's transformative work in our lives.

In keeping with her usual style in practically all of her three previous writings, Kuukua ends this work on a high note that brings it all home with a collection of amazing testimonies from testifiers from all walks of life: Beauty therapists, Sanctuary keepers, drivers, lawyers, retirees, Montessori teachers, media program specialists, homemakers, entrepreneurs, the unemployed, teachers, and the list goes on!

This book will bless you - Period!!!

Guard Your Heart boldly confronts us with our hypocrisy and religious spirits and challenges us to pay attention to many other critical, but often overlooked attitudes that poison our relationship with our life-giving Source. Over and above that, it gives us the needed road map that will aid us to *guard our hearts* to save our souls. When Kuukua sent me the manuscript of *Guard Your Heart* and graciously invited me to review it, the Spirit of God whispered to me, *"You are doing this more for you, than for her!"*

As always, He was bang on point!!!

Reading *Guard Your Heart* has been for me, both an exhilarating and deeply reflective experience. It has, I believe, purified my motives, and ignited in me a burning desire for a heart like His (i.e., Jesus). It has reminded me to major on the majors and minor on the minors. Most importantly, it has reprogrammed me to a new default setting.......W-W-J-D!

I pray it does the same for you!

[*W-W-J-D. - What Would Jesus Do?]

- Patrick Masoperh

"Above all else, guard your heart, for everything you do, flows from it."

Proverbs 4:23 NIV

DEDICATION

This book is dedicated to: Rev. Mrs. Abena Boamah Asare.

Osofo, I dedicate this book to you.
You are the vessel the Lord chose to baptize me in the Holy Spirit. I am eternally grateful to you and your family.
God bless you.

ACKNOWLEDGEMENTS

I thank each and every person who has contributed to the production of this book.

May God bless you all!

TABLE OF CONTENTS

Reviews — iii
Dedication — xii
Acknowledgements — xiii
Foreword — xvi
Preface — xviii
Introduction — xx
Chapter Prelude — xxii

PART ONE

Chapter 1:: How Did I Get Here? — 1
Chapter 2:: The Problem with Self-Entitlement — 7
Chapter 3:: Ingratitude Comes in Many Forms — 13
Chapter 4:: Stop Fighting Me in Your Head — 17
Chapter 5:: What About the Positives? — 20
Chapter 6:: Focus On Substance and Not Form — 22
Chapter 7:: And So What?! — 26
Chapter 8:: All It Took Was a Text Message — 30
Chapter 9:: Watch Out (A three-in-one story) — 33
Chapter 10:: Offence In the Sight of God — 41
Chapter 11:: What A Test! — 45
Chapter 12:: The Cancer of Pride and Ego — 49
Chapter 13:: Food — 54

PART TWO

Reflection — 58
Chapter Prelude — 61
Chapter 14:: Hope Deferred Makes the Heart Sick — 62
Chapter 15:: My Flesh my Enemy — 71
Chapter 16:: Heart Cleansing (1) — 79
Chapter 17:: Heart Cleansing (2) — 87

Chapter 18:: Guard Your Heart	**93**
Chapter 19:: Guard Your Heart And Your Tongue	**99**

PART THREE
Chapter Prelude	**106**
Chapter 20:: Do Penance	**108**
Chapter 21:: He Is Not Talking To Someone	**112**
Chapter 22:: Forgiveness Saves The Soul	**115**
Chapter 23:: Let It Go	**120**
Chapter 24:: "Keep a Clean Heart, I Will Do The Rest"	**122**
Chapter 25:: Cantankerous? Never gain!	**125**
Chapter 26:: The Journey to Truly Loving My Mother	**127**

Conclusion	**130**
Biography of Victoria Twum-Gyamrah	**131**

FOREWORD

I am honoured to write the foreword to Kuukua's fourth book, *Guard Your Heart* co-authored with Victoria Twum-Gyamrah, her mentee. I have had no desire to put down the manuscript ever since I received it. I can closely relate to the two disciples on the road to Emmaus in Luke 24:32 who after their encounter with Jesus said, *"Were not our hearts burning within us while he talked with us on the road and opened the Scriptures to us?"*

In my case, my heart burned with conviction as I viewed my life through the lens of this book. Kuukua and Victoria give a detailed, spiritual account of how certain sins can clog our hearts. We tend to justify them, but these sins are most likely the reason why our lives can be barren and unfruitful in spite of fasting, prayer and seed-sowing in the face of trying circumstances.

Kuukua and Victoria identify issues such as self-entitlement, ingratitude, bitterness, anger, and having a critical spirit as reasons for losing out on God's best in life. They admonish the reader, with the help of the Holy Spirit, to repent of these sins and experience breakthroughs where they have struggled to see change for many years.

The personal testimonies of the authors and those of others, vividly expose to the reader, the adverse effect of these issues on their lives. As they repent, the transformed life is just as clear. Kuukua tells the story in a most refreshing style. Victoria's *food for thought* dovetails beautifully with Kuukua's script, which is a sure sign that mentorship is more caught than taught.

Guard Your Heart is a must-read for every believer who is seeking to go past the *"same old, same old"* walk and desires to remould their heart into a sanctuary for God. What is of the utmost importance to Him is the condition of a man's heart. When God sent the Prophet Samuel to anoint one of Jesse's sons as king, Samuel was impressed when he saw Eliab step forward. At that point, Samuel concluded that Eliab was God's anointed. The words of I Samuel 16:7 are most instructive: *"But the LORD said to Samuel, 'Do not be impressed by his appearance or his height, for I have rejected him. God does not view things the way people do. People look on the outward appearance, but the LORD looks at the heart.'"* (New English Translation)

The journey to rid our hearts of offence will not be an easy one. There will be pain and setbacks, and at times we may want to give up. Do not give up. Be encouraged. Set your eyes on the prize, and you will discover God's best version of yourself when you allow the Holy Spirit to do a deep work in your heart. As you read and seek His face, be assured that He comforts while He does His work of transformation.

- *Daniel Kobla Glymin May 2024 Accra, Ghana*

PREFACE

Over the past year, the Holy Spirit has been taking me on a journey where the heart is concerned.

In Proverbs 4:23, we are cautioned to guard our hearts diligently because everything we do flows from the heart. This presupposes whether we live a victorious life or not is not dependent on God or our prayers. It is dependent on the condition of our hearts.

Unfortunately, I doubt many Christians have taken the pains to study what the scriptures say about the heart and made any attempts to diligently keep our hearts. At least, I sure do know I had not, until just recently when the Holy Spirit started drawing my attention to this issue.

The Holy Spirit has enjoined me to discuss a few things He has taught me pertaining to how those of us who profess Christ create a conducive atmosphere for the enemy, the accuser of the brethren to gain access into our lives.

In this book, you will be reading some of the interesting revelations the Holy Spirit has taught me on this matter.

I have also shared a few testimonies generated from some of the meetings I have had in the course of the year on this topic.

I hope that this book will enlighten you and help you to life-changing decisions that will benefit your generations.

INTRODUCTION

This book is divided into three main parts. In the first part of the book, I introduce my life's journey and share a few personal experiences where the Holy Spirit rebuked me and drew my attention to the state of my heart. Each experience is, in turn, followed by food for thought written by Victoria, one of my mentees, and a co-author of this book. I also share an important lesson I have learnt from my spiritual father, Archbishop Nicholas Duncan Williams, on pride.

In the second part of the book, I talk briefly about some of the meetings I was invited to speak at in relation to deferred hope, anger, and heart cleansing. I further share a few testimonies from only two people from each of the meetings. These testifiers recount the meetings and the effect they had on them.

In the third part, I share testimonies of a few readers of my first book *"An Available Vessel for the Lord's Pleasure,"* these are testimonies that were shared at my 'Meet the Author Series' meetings between October 2023 and April 2024.

I hope that each story and/or testimony shared in this book

will touch you and help you pay attention to the state of your heart as a professed child of Christ.

PART ONE

CHAPTER PRELUDE

As of the time I am writing this book, I can say boldly and confidently that to the best of my knowledge, I do not bear anyone a grudge, I am not holding anyone to strict account in my heart due to pain caused me, anger, bitterness, or offence. Over the past few years, the Holy Spirit has brought to my remembrance people that I had been angry with and therefore held in my heart and He has helped me to release all of them, year in, year out.

I believe it is for this reason that He has permitted me to share some of my experiences with you with the hope that a testimony, a revelation and or some of the lessons I have learnt and would share would help you guard your heart and set you free.

I share these stories in no particular order of importance. There is no pattern to it. However, I am sure that the Holy Spirit Himself would weave them together in a very beautiful way to convict you of the need to guard your heart to save your soul.

CHAPTER 1

HOW DID I GET HERE?

I was born to Mr. Allswell Kojo Awotwi and Ms. Josephine Amissah-Arthur on 19th June 1974. When I was three years old, I was sent to my grandparents at Oda where my Grandpa was the headmaster of Oda Secondary School[1].

When he retired, we moved to Cape Coast, this is where I had my primary and secondary school education. I attended the University Primary[2] and Wesley Girls' High Schools[3] respectively.

At Wesley Girls' High School, I became a member of the school's drama club. Just before we were done with our 'A' level exams, the National Theatre Players, then *Abibigromma*[4] of Ghana came to enact a play in the school. A couple of my friends and I took advantage of the situation and requested the leaders of the group to allow us to do our National

---

1 *Oda Secondary school, now Oda Senior High School, is a co-educational second-cycle institution in Akim Oda, situated in the Birim Central Municipal District in the Eastern Region of Ghana*
2 *University primary school is the primary arm of the University of Cape-Coast*
3 *Wesley Girls' High School, now Wesley Girls' Senior High School is a second-cycle institute for girls located in Cape-Coast Ghana*
4 *National Drama Company (Formerly Abibigromma) is a theatre group in Ghana*

Service with them. That is how I found myself thrown into the entertainment industry at an early age. I did my one-year National Service[5] with the Theatre Players and went on to work with the Director of Theatre Operations of the National Theatre[6] for two more years.

After my secondary education, I entered the University of Ghana[7] to read law, and subsequently to the Ghana School of Law to obtain my law certificate. On 4th October, 2002, I was called to the Ghana Bar.

When I finished law school, I served my second National service at the Attorney General's Department in Koforidua, in the Eastern Region of the Republic of Ghana. Later, I joined a private legal firm and worked with them for three years. After my third year at the firm, I moved on to public service. I worked with the Ghana Immigration Service[8], and later the Petroleum Commission[9] for a total of eight years before I started my legal firm KuukuaA Legal Consulting with my husband.

When I was growing up, I attended the Wesley Methodist Church in Cape Coast with my grandparents. Since Wesley Girls' High School was also a Methodist school, I considered myself an Orthodox Christian.

However, a few days before my 21st birthday, I had an

---

5 *National Service is a mandatory one-year period of service to the state for tertiary school leavers.*
6 *Ghana's foremost theatre edifice for performance and theatre programs management.*
7 *University of Ghana is Ghana's premiere university, located in Legon, Accra Ghana.*
8 *The Ghana Immigration Service, under the Ministry of the Interior, regulates visa, entry, and residence permit applications in Ghana.*
9 *The Petroleum Commission is the upstream oil and gas regulator in Ghana mandated to regulate, manage, and coordinate upstream petroleum activities.*

encounter with the Lord at the Lighthouse Chapel International[10] at Korle-Gonno in Accra. On this day the Holy Spirit convicted me, and I gave my life to Christ. However, that was all I did and for nine years I stayed at that church but did not submit to discipleship classes nor to any form of leadership. I was just a churchgoer.

After working with the Ghana Immigration Service for nine years, everything changed when I attended a prayer meeting at Sunny FM called "Lunchtime Prayers." It was held between 12 noon and 2:00 pm and was open to anyone in the area who wanted to pray. It was during these prayer meetings that I began to learn about the spiritual gifts and the workings of the Holy Spirit. It was at this prayer meeting that I met certain key people who changed the course of my Christian walk: Auntie Leah Nicole, of blessed memory, Rev. Abena Asare[11], to whom this book is dedicated, and Apostle Dan Clad[12].

I joined the Asbury Dunwell Church[13] after leaving the Lighthouse Chapel International. At this fellowship which also had a Methodist flair, I met two more people who would be instrumental in my spiritual journey and growth. Reverend Paul Adu[14] my mentor of blessed memory, and Mr. Kobla Glymin[15].

---

10 Lighthouse Chapel International is a charismatic church founded by Bishop Dag Heward-Mills, it is now known as the United Denomination (Lighthouse Group of Churches).
11 Rev. Abena Asare, is the founder of Ladies of Substance International Network (LOSIN).
12 Apostle Dan Clad is the Head Pastor and Founder of Ablaze Chapel International.
13 Asbury Dunwell Church is a Christian congregation located on the independence avenue in Accra, Ghana
14 Rev. Paul Adu Jnr., my mentor of blessed memory. He was the resident minister at St. Peter Methodist Society, Mile 7, New Achimota, Accra, Ghana.
15 Kobla Glymin Esq: A lawyer and a friend.

In 2011, I read a book by Dave Roberson titled *The Walk of the Spirit, The Walk of Power, The Vital Role of Speaking in Tongues*. That year, I learnt a lot about how to develop a personal relationship with the Holy Spirit. Above all, I learnt how praying in tongues makes a Christian a more effective prayer warrior. I discovered that the more I prayed in tongues, the more the Holy Spirit communicated with my inner self. As a result, the Holy Spirit worked through me to help me mortify my flesh and become more like Christ every day.

The foremost thing I learnt was how praying in tongues creates a channel of communication between you and the Holy Spirit. By this channel of communication, the Holy Spirit who was present when God was creating you downloads God's original purpose and intent into your spirit and your inner man and helps you to live a fulfilled God driven, purposeful life. This new passion for prayer would lead me to many wonderful testimonies!

Also, a few years ago I got introduced to the Full Gospel Business Men's Fellowship (FGBMFI). For the better part of my life, I had assumed that it was a fellowship for only men. I was mistaken. It was when I joined the fellowship a few years ago that I understood why the Lord in the last decade had taken me through some painful processes, it was to give me this platform to enable me to share my testimonies and to encourage the body of Christ. I understood that I was finally home, for indeed, I had bagged several testimonies that I could share to impact the body of Christ.

Still on the topic of testimonies, as I grew in intimacy with the Holy Spirit, on May 1, 2022, I launched my first book,

An Available Vessel for the Lord's Pleasure. It is a collection of over sixty powerful testimonies which demonstrates the power of the Holy Spirit in the life of a believer. In the book I share stories from my childhood, my career, and my intimate relationship with the Holy Spirit. My greatest desire for every reader of *An Available Vessel for the Lord's Pleasure* is to develop a personal relationship with the Holy Ghost. This desire was borne from an observation I had made in my Christian life. I had noticed that many Christians within my circles loved to read the Bible and to pray, but not many truly knew or understood the role of the Holy Spirit in their lives as Christians.

In 2023 I published my second book *Did I Bear Fruits?* In that book, I have a collection of testimonies from people who had read the book *An Available Vessel for the Lord's Pleasure.* They share the testimonies, experiences, and life-changing decisions they made after reading the book. Ultimately after reading *Did I Bear Fruits?* the question I want people to ask is, did I bear fruits after my kind? Was I able to get other believers to desire an intimate relationship with the Holy Spirit like I did when I read *The Walk of the Holy Spirit, The Walk of Power?* Was I able to raise many an available vessel for the Lord's pleasure? That is what the book *Did I Bear Fruits?* is about. It can be described as a sequel to *An Available Vessel for the Lord's Pleasure.* It is a collection of testimonies from testifiers from varied backgrounds: Drivers, men of God, homemakers, lawyers, entrepreneurs, unemployed people, students, teachers, bankers et al.

In the same year 2023, I published my third book The *Benefits of Obeying 'Nonsense.'* In that book the Holy Spirit directed me to share a few testimonies on some of the experiences I have had with Him, particularly some personal testimonies of instructions He gave me that did not make sense, and yet when I obeyed, the results were mind-blowing.

The book also has testimonies of other people who have had similar experiences because they either heard me share a testimony or two about obeying instructions that did not make sense, or I taught them how to obey instructions that did not make sense and eventually they have come to appreciate that unique relationship with the Holy Spirit.

The testimonies shared in that book will increase your faith and assure you of the presence of the Holy Spirit in your life, if you have accepted the Lord Jesus as your personal Saviour and encourage you to develop a more intimate relationship with Him. You will no longer doubt that the Holy Spirit has been speaking with, through and to you when you thought whatever you kept hearing was nonsense.

This has been the journey to my fourth book, *Guard Your Heart* which you hold in your hands. I hope you enjoy the read.

CHAPTER 2

THE PROBLEM WITH SELF-ENTITLEMENT

A few years ago, I had the rare privilege of being introduced to His Excellency John Dramani Mahama.[16] At the time he was the Member of Parliament for Bole Bamboi[17]. Over the years my relationship with him extended to his wife, his siblings and almost all the members of his family. In fact, his brothers refer to me as their little sister.

When His Excellency became president, I was working at the Petroleum Commission, and the Chief Executive Officer Dr. Donkor resigned to contest as a Member of Parliament for the Pru[18] Constituency. He won and went on to become the Member of Parliament. This meant that the position for the CEO had to be filled.

Up until now, I am not too sure why I felt that I was the right person to replace Dr. Donkor[19]. When His Excellency

---

16 John Dramani Mahama is a Ghanaian politician who served as President of Ghana from 24 July 2012 to 7 January 2017.
17 Bole or Bole-Bamboi is one of the constituencies represented in the Parliament of Ghana. Bole is located in the Bole district of the Savannah Region of Ghana.
18 Pru East is one of the constituencies represented in the Parliament of Ghana, it was created in 2004. Pru East is in the Bono East Region of Ghana.
19 Dr Donkor is a Ghanaian politician and a former Minister for Power. He is the cur-

asked me who I thought could become the chief executive, I expressed interest. For some reason, he didn't say yes, and he didn't say no. The decision dragged on for so long that at a point it became a problem between the two of us. I felt that if he didn't want to make me the chief executive he should just say so. Even though he didn't tell me exactly why he didn't think I was suitable for the position, he just didn't say anything until one day he appointed someone else.

Clearly, I was very upset! In hindsight, that was really arrogant because I still don't know why I felt that I was the most important person who had to occupy that position. That is the problem with being self-entitled or with self-entitlement. I am sure that this feeling was fuelled by the kind of relationship I had with him and his family members, but that didn't mean he had to appoint me to that position.

That is not the end of the story. A few years after this incident, I had moved on, started my family, and set up my law firm, and between myself and His Excellency, we had not talked about that appointment issue again. In fact, at a point he had even appointed me to be a Board Member of EDAIF (Export Trade, Agricultural and Industrial Development Fund), now Exim Bank[20]. As far as I was concerned, this issue was behind us. However, a few years ago I had gone for a prayer meeting at my church Action Chapel International[21] dubbed Morning Glory[22] which is from 5:30 am- 6:30 am

---

rent Member of Parliament for the Pru East constituency, in the Bono East Region of Ghana.

20   EXIM Bank- The Ghana Export-Import Bank is the principal export finance institution of the Government of Ghana.
21   Action Chapel International- A Charismatic Christian church based in Accra, Ghana. The church was founded by Nicholas Duncan-Williams in 1979, It is the headquarters of Christian Action Faith Ministries (CAFM).
22   Morning Glory is a prayer meeting held early in the mornings at the Action Chapel

every weekday. Just as I knelt at the altar I heard *'Release John from your heart! Release John from your heart.'*

I was taken aback when the Holy Spirit said that to me because I didn't think that I was holding him to strict account in my heart. In fact, we were fine and there was no issue. This matter I am talking about happened so many years ago, more than eight years ago. I didn't know why the Holy Spirit was telling me to release him from account in my heart. Then He said to me, *'The day you talk about him and tears don't well up in your eyes, that is the day you would have released him from your heart.'* That was very interesting because it was the first time I realised that any time I spoke about His Excellency, anytime I had a discussion with anybody and his name came up, somehow tears would well up in my eyes. But there was no way I could have imagined that it was because I still felt pain from that incident! So, I prayed, asked for forgiveness, and made the decision to release him from account in my heart.

Two days later I was with a group of people having a discussion after a Full Gospel[23] meeting. The discussion touched on politics and his administration. We spoke a lot about his administration and his appointments among other things and then I went home. It was when I was ready to go to bed that night that the Holy Spirit whispered, *'Now you have released him from account in your heart, for the first time, tears did not well up in your eyes when you spoke about him.'*

Cathedral, Accra.
23 The Full Gospel Business Men's Fellowship International is a fellowship of lay businessmen and women. Its main purpose is to bring interest to the Christian gospel. Theologically, the organization has its roots in Pentecostalism. See fgbmfi.org

I share this story because it was an especially important lesson I learnt that day. It meant you could be on good terms with somebody who had offended you, somebody you had a problem with, yet you wouldn't even know that you were holding the person in your heart. As far as I was concerned, this issue happened, and we had settled it. I thought I had moved on and we were fine. But apparently, deep inside I still felt offended and I still had pain from that incident.

As I sat and reflected on it, I asked myself *"Why was I even upset about the matter?"* It was his prerogative to appoint anyone that he wanted, so why was I so upset? And why did I feel such pain? And why was I offended? I realized that the only reason why I felt that way was because I felt self-entitled due to the relationship I had with him, and this was a very big lesson for me. A lesson I hope everyone reading this book will learn: the problem with self-entitlement.

Food for thought

How many times do we reason things out with the wisdom of the world?

Reading this experience my mind is drawn to the many wise sayers, motivational speakers and even some preachers who may use a similar occurrence to teach us how to handle situations where our expectations were not met.

Teaching things like 'operate wisely!' 'See people for who they are!' 'Be alert!' 'How to identify your people!' etc. These are all well and good yet no mention is made of the possible problem of self-arrogance, nor self-entitlement?!

These are the unseen diseases that are eating up our hearts and thoughts. Consuming our hearts in insidious ways, soon we justify feelings of hurt and rationalize why we must feel the way we do.

When we approach situations with the mindset of the world and take advice from worldly wisdom, we may end up making decisions that do not align with our values or beliefs. Over time, this can lead to a gradual build-up of iniquity in our hearts and minds. We may begin to compromise on our principles and make choices that are not in line with our true selves.

As we continue down this path, we may find it increasingly difficult to recognize our own values and beliefs, and we may even lose sight of who we truly are. We need to choose the wisdom of God, and that is only known by the Holy Spirit.

It doesn't matter how long it has been since an incident happened, anytime it comes to mind or you are ever reminded of it, ask the

Holy Spirit about it. It is prudent to ask the Holy Spirit what He is saying with that situation of hurt you may be feeling right now or may have gone through. That situation of disappointment from the person you were SO sure would come through for you, ask the Holy Spirit what He is saying to you through these experiences.

Is He pointing out self-entitlement, overdependence on human strength, bitterness, pride, and arrogant issues? Is He asking for a release of the pain and the individual from account in your heart? Chew on that for a moment.

In the same vein let us all be careful of the lessons we learn from people's experiences; 'iniquity' has been repackaged and sold as motivational messages and even sermons. Always seek the Holy Spirit.

CHAPTER 3

INGRATITUDE COMES IN MANY FORMS

I had a problem with one of my aunties. This is a woman who had been there for me for most of my life. Because I was not on good terms with my biological mother whilst growing up, this aunty was there for me anytime I needed someone to speak to or needed to speak to a mother figure. In fact, many people thought she was my biological mother. Anywhere that we would go, she would introduce me as her daughter.

A few years ago, something happened that strained the relationship. I stopped going to visit her, and I stopped telling her things about my personal life, this is something that I used to do with her. There was nothing that I wouldn't discuss with her. I sought her opinion on almost everything that I would do, but this issue strained the relationship and I basically stopped talking to her.

One day, I was going to drop my kids at school and just when I was backing out of the house I heard *'Remember she has fed you before, remember she has fed you before.'* Immediately the Holy Spirit started ministering to me and drew my attention to how ingratitude penetrates the heart. He drew my attention and made me reflect on everything this woman had done for me over the years. He drew my attention to how I had allowed other people's commentary on the matter between us to influence me, and I had turned my back on the one person who had been there for me for years. And He said *'Ingratitude comes in many forms.'*

Is there someone who has been there for you for many years, yet you have turned your back on simply because of a misunderstanding?

Could you reflect on the relationship? Please apologise, make amends, and ask for forgiveness!

Food for thought

Sometimes, if not all the time, I have come to realise that the Holy Spirit speaks with the simplest things. We on the other hand are sometimes caught up seeking the big things and we become complicated beings! We overthink! How ironic, God in His 'Supreme Complexity' is still simple in dealing with us. Yet we, with our simple ways seek to be more complex than God. We overthink!

Let us pause and reflect on the instructions here. She was instructed to remember a time when this person had been there for her, and not offend that hand that fed her at a point in her life, simple.

You see, I believe this is because anyone who extends a gracious hand to you, is being moved by the Holy Spirit! Yep, it has nothing to do with our cool personalities…it has everything to do with God! As I type this my mind is flooded by all the many moments in my life when people have done 'little' acts of grace towards me. The people God used to help me through school, the aunts and uncles who gave monies to support my education. I had an aunt who provided me with provisions for the four years I was an undergraduate. Wow! My big sisters and brothers who passed by to visit me, paid a hostel fee and called me to check up on me.

The 'strangers' who gave me opportunities to work in their organisations and trusted me without work experience when all others sought work experience of five years! The friends who showed up just on birthdays with just the right message of encouragement, the friend who got me a copy of An Available Vessel for the Lord's Pleasure! There are many, many moments.

And guess what, He doesn't just use Christians to bless us. The sovereignty of God is not limited to working with just a group of people, I believe that God will use who or what is available. If He can use a donkey, He can use anyone!

It may have been a simple hot meal when you didn't have one.... most often it is something as simple as that, yet it was the 'hand' you needed at the moment! To forget these moments and act in anger or bitterness when relationships go sour or pained, despising those moments is equal to saying, 'I despise the help you gave to me at that time God'...wow, indeed our actions of ingratitude shout louder than our words of 'Praise the Lord!!'

You may be saying as you read this, "You do not know what the person did, if you did you would understand." You are right I do not know what the person did or said to make you regret ever taking anything from the person or even knowing him or her. But God KNOWS, in fact, GOD KNEW even before whatever caused a falling out between you and the person. GOD KNOWS ALL THINGS. And the same GOD says LET IT GO, HE KNOWS SOMETHING WE DO NOT KNOW! Let us Obey!

CHAPTER 4

STOP FIGHTING ME IN YOUR HEAD

Several years ago, I was in a relationship with a very mature man. In fact, he was very wise. I am not too sure exactly what happened that made us start fighting a lot. I had issues with almost everything that he did. He just had to say one thing, I would take it out of context, mull over it, complain, rant, rave, and go on and on and on about it.

One day he came to visit me and I started ranting about something that he had done. After I had talked and talked for over fifteen to twenty minutes he quietly said, *'Stop fighting me in your head.'* A few months later we broke up.

Years later I met someone who knew both of us and the person asked me a question that made me sit back and reflect on that relationship. The person asked me how we broke up, and it was the first time I had to sit and reflect on the relationship and actually find out why we broke up. That is when I remembered what he told me years ago *'Stop fighting me in your head.'*

As I reflected, I realized that anytime he said something I

didn't like I would stand in front of a mirror, go over what he said, I would make an argument out of it, then I would imagine what his response would be, attack that response and then argue it out! I would sit and think of what I would say next, imagine what he would say next and my response to that! I would go on and on like this for minutes, whilst standing in front of the mirror.

That is when I realized that the day he said *'Stop fighting me in your head'* he knew what I had been doing, and he knew that we really did not have a problem, but it was because I just wouldn't let the simple things that were wrong with the relationship go. I had to go over them over and over again until they became magnified beyond reason.

Perhaps you have been doing the same. Is it possible that you really don't have a problem in your relationship but it is just because you have been fighting your partner in your head?

Have you been going over something they said that offended you and making a big case out of it when it is really not a big case? Please stop fighting your partner, stop fighting him, stop fighting her in your head!!!.

Food for thought

I have encountered this pattern of behaviour not only in romantic relationships but also in various aspects of my life where I feel the need to anticipate and prepare myself for every possible outcome. However, as I am growing in my walk with the Holy Spirit, I have come to realize that such acts of preparation and anticipation can erode my ability to trust God in the moments when I need it the most.

In relationships, constantly preparing for the worst-case scenario takes away from the freedom of being yourself in every moment and simply trusting God.

It's understandable to feel overwhelmed and anxious in uncertain situations, but instead of dwelling on the worst-case scenario, why not turn to the Lord who is love? By putting your trust in Him, you can be assured that no matter what challenges come your way, He will guide you through them. His love is unconditional, and His grace is sufficient to carry you through any circumstance. So, let go of your worries and have faith in the Lord who is always faithful and true.

CHAPTER 5

WHAT ABOUT THE POSITIVES?

My husband has an attitude that really irritates me, over the years it has been the source of many discussions and arguments. One day I went to the Lord very frustrated complaining and praying. After I had finished praying, I just heard *'What about the positives?'* in a very very small voice. *'What about the positives?'* So, I repeated the question *'What about the positives?'* Then He said, *"You have been complaining about this habit for so long, what about his other positive attributes?"* I was dumbstruck.

That was when I realised how much time I had spent complaining about the habit and had even forgotten or not reflected on any of his positive attributes. It was a very, very, good lesson. *What about the positives?*

Anytime you are tempted to complain about your spouse, your boss, your colleague, your parents, your siblings, a schoolmate, or a classmate, could you pause for just a minute, and ask *"What about the positives?"* Could you try and focus on the positives of the person instead of the few negatives that bother you so much? *What about the positives?*

Food for thought

I believe that we often forget that the love of the Lord is abundant and reaches everyone, even those who we believe should be on His list of naughty kids because they may have hurt or offended us.

It is common knowledge that being in a long-term relationship can be challenging at times. Even the happiest of couples have their moments of irritation and frustration with each other. However, recent studies have shown that the person who can easily irritate and offend you the most is often your spouse. This phenomenon can be attributed to the fact that we tend to be more open and honest with our partners, the proximity and constant interaction with our spouses can make 'small annoyances' seem magnified, making us lose sight of the beautifully crafted positives.

If only we could see people as God sees them, we would be more tolerant and less judgmental. I mean we never ever possibly love a person more than God loves that person, He sees ALL their flaws, yet He loves them completely!

He died for us whilst we were yet sinners Romans 5:8 "But God demonstrates His own love toward us, in that while we were still sinners, Christ died for us."

Beloved, let us pray for the grace to practice the love that has been deposited in us, let us pray for the grace to work out love as God love's: through the lens of eternal Love-Christ.

CHAPTER 6

FOCUS ON SUBSTANCE NOT FORM

A few months ago, the Holy Spirit laid it on my heart to organise a retreat for a group of ladies and He said I should introduce the topic of heart cleansing. During one Saturday evening prayer meeting held over the Zoom App, one of the leaders asked if I would like to speak a little more about the topic and what we planned to do at the retreat.

I was so excited, and for about fifteen minutes I proceeded to share with them some of the lessons I had learnt in the year; what the Holy Spirit had been teaching me about some of the things that we do that give the enemy access to our lives and block our prayers from being answered. I used Psalm 66:18 which says *'if I regard iniquity in my heart the Lord will not hear me,'* I drew attention to Psalm 51:10-12, I talked about how at the retreat we must pray and ask the Lord to create a new heart and renew a right spirit within us. I referred to Proverbs 4:23 as well. I was so excited! I used about four examples from my own experiences and I thought they were very excited and looking forward to the retreat.

The next day I got a message from one of the leaders. Amidst other things, the message relayed that some of the people who had joined the prayer line the day before indicated that I didn't thank them for coming online to pray.

When I read the message, I was dumbfounded. Suddenly the Holy Spirit started ministering to me, saying *'Do you now understand why I chose that topic? Do you understand why I said to have a retreat to teach them some of the things I have been teaching you? Whilst you were excited and passionately talking about the things that block the heart which allows the enemy to gain access to you and some of the reasons why probably their problems have not been answered, all someone was interested in was thank you. Everything that you said was lost on some of them. Do you now see? All that they were interested in was for you to tell them thank you for coming online to pray. How significant is that in relation to the assignment I have given you where they are concerned? Do you see? This is one of the reasons why I have asked you to organise the retreat and talk to them about some of the things that block their prayers.'*

'She didn't even say thank you!' Can you imagine?

What are you focused on? Are you focused on things that tickle your ego, or are you paying attention to the things that will build you up and edify you?

Please focus on substance, not form!!!

Food for thought:

Love.

This word is not reserved for only romantic relationships, it is supposed to be our general approach to life and people... stay with me on this I am getting somewhere with this...

Love is not something we should always focus on receiving, it is rather what we are to give at all times. I once listened to a Kenneth Hagin's[24] sermon, where he shared a testimony, I have paraphrased here: A woman who had had issues with her family approached him for prayer and he counselled her to 'walk in love' and forgive all persons who had hurt her and actually work out love by showing love and practising love towards all who she previously held in her heart. She did so and gradually began to 'walk in love.' A few months later he was back in that part of town preaching again and there was an urgent call for him to come to this very same woman's house to pray for her daughter who had a severe seizure.

Kenneth Hagin recounts that the Holy Spirit instructed him not to pray for the child when he got to the house. When he arrived at the home the Holy Spirit told him to tell the woman to command the seizure to cease by saying 'Devil, take your hands off my daughter for I am walking in love!" The woman made this command and immediately her daughter was free!
The power of love!

You may be asking what the connection is between this testimony and the one you just read? Love must be in all we do, that is the connection. Listen in love, eat in love, dance in love, read in

---

[24] *Kenneth Hagin 1917-2003, was a Pentecostal evangelist and pastor who founded Rhema Bible Church and Bible College in Tulsa, Oklahoma. He was a dynamic teacher, preacher, and prophet, with teachings on the Faith and the power of the Holy Spirit.*

love, speak in love! Walk in love everyday. Stop being petty, it is not love, it is bitterness! Please let us stop excusing our "crappy" behaviour with traditional expectations. Situate cultural and moral lessons in love, teaching generations to walk in love, to the young and the elderly. Do not just accord people what tradition, and culture demand. You see, all things may fail and offend, but where love is, there is no offence!

Oh, and just so you know, and to give a foundation, love is not a 'spiritualised' 'whooshie' 'whooshy' feeling! No please, love is Christ!

CHAPTER 7

AND SO WHAT?!

I didn't know my father when I was growing up. I didn't even have a mental image of how he looked like. When I turned twenty-one, I set out on an expedition to look for him and I found him. Interestingly the first thing he said when he saw me was *'Kuukua, I knew you would come.'*

For a second, I wondered how he knew it was me, but of course, everyone says I look exactly like my mother so I don't think it was that difficult for him to recognise who I was.

After I found him, I resolved to spend the next several years taking care of him. I made it a point to send him groceries and pocket money every month. Anytime he had to go to the hospital I would take him and take care of the hospital bills. When he died in 2010, I made sure he had a befitting burial, and many people were amazed.

In this book, we are talking about some of the issues and some of the ways the enemy gets access into our lives. We all know what the bible says about honour: *"honour your father and your mother so that it will be well with you, and you will live long."* My father didn't take care of me, I didn't even know him, and so what?

Ephesians 6:2-3 *"Honour your father and mother, (which is the first commandment with promise) that it may be well with you, and you may live long on the earth."*

I have heard many people who are very bitter because a parent didn't take care of them. What I always tell such people is that it takes an egg and a sperm to form a human being.

Irrespective of the fact that your father didn't take care of you, but for his sperm, you wouldn't be a human being. Irrespective of the fact that your mother didn't take care of you but for her egg, you would not be here. Let me ask you a question. Do you fall within the category of someone whose parents didn't take care of? *And so what?*

At the end of the day anytime you hold on to this bitterness and this pain, you are actually breaking scripture. You are not honouring your parents! Do not be surprised if your prayers are hardly answered or you have many troubles in your life.

At this stage, I would like you to pause and think very carefully. Do you even know why your father did not take care of you? Do you know why your mother walked away and didn't even look back? Have you bothered to put yourself in their shoes? AND SO WHAT? They didn't take care of you, AND SO WHAT?

Please make amends, release them from your heart and put yourself in their shoes. As a child of God, ask yourself *'What would Jesus expect of me?'*

Food for thought

I have come to believe that one of the greatest show of love, is to honour! I know it's easy to honour what is good and lovely! It is expected actually, to honour what is nice and lovely and good, I mean it's almost a piece of cake affair! It is effortless to recognize and acknowledge things that please us. However, it takes effort to appreciate and honour things that are not so easy to deal with, such as challenges, struggles, and hardships. It is human nature to avoid things that are difficult and uncomfortable, but recognizing and honouring these issues is crucial for spiritual growth and development. Hmm, now the true test of honour is when you are required to honour the 'bad' and 'ugly'! Ah ha! Then the excuses begin, and we list all the many reasons why we shouldn't do what Love requires us to do!

It takes a conscious effort to appreciate and acknowledge the efforts and struggles of others who are dealing with difficult situations. We tend to overlook the hard work that goes into overcoming challenges. Honouring both the good and the difficult is essential for personal growth and development. It helps us become more empathetic, understanding, and compassionate towards those around us and ourselves. It allows us to look inward and reflect on our own lives, experiences, and struggles, and to find meaning and purpose in them.

You see, the test is not to love the person who 'deserves' love… the test is in loving the 'undeserved.' These are not my words oo if you don't believe me, you can check out (Luke 6:27-36) where Jesus said it!

"But I say to you who hear: Love your enemies, do good to those who hate you, bless those who curse you, and pray for those who spitefully use you. To him who strikes you on the one cheek, offer

the other also. And from him who takes away your cloak, do not withhold your tunic either. Give to everyone who asks of you. And from him who takes away your goods do not ask them back. And just as you want men to do to you, you also do to them likewise.

But if you love those who love you, what credit is that to you? For even sinners love those who love them. And if you do good to those who do good to you, what credit is that to you? For even sinners do the same. And if you lend to those from whom you hope to receive back, what credit is that to you? For even sinners lend to sinners to receive as much back. But love your enemies, do good, and lend, [a]hoping for nothing in return; and your reward will be great, and you will be sons of the Most High. For He is kind to the unthankful and evil. Therefore, be merciful, just as your Father also is merciful" (Luke 27-36).

CHAPTER 8

ALL IT TOOK WAS A TEXT MESSAGE

At age twenty-two I married my childhood sweetheart. I had been in a relationship with him throughout my teenage years. The marriage lasted for approximately three years then I broke it off. For the next ten years, the two of us were at loggerheads.

Interestingly he worked in the same organisation as one of my sisters and he lived in the same country with another sister of mine. My sisters were in touch with him, but I wasn't. Inadvertently, however, I had an idea about what was going on in his life.

One day I thought to myself, *'What kind of childish behaviour is this?'* I got his number from one of my sisters and I sent him a simple text message saying, *'Can we stop behaving like two spoilt kids and behave more maturely.'* It took no longer than five minutes, he replied and said, *'Even two spoilt children would not behave so badly, can I call you?'* He called. We spoke for over an hour as though the last ten years had not existed, and we have been in contact up to now.

All it took was a simple text message to break ten years of unnecessary heartache and pain. What would have happened if I hadn't sent that text message, I have always wondered. Ever since then we have remained friends.

What is the relationship between you and your ex? Are you bitter? Are you in pain? Are you still holding a grudge? Are you angry? Maybe like me, all it will take is a text message to resolve the problem. Are you bold enough to take that step as a child of God to ensure that your heart is free of pain, anger, and bitterness?

Take that step!

Food for thought

Let's think about the times and seasons! People may come into our lives for times and seasons and then fade away. People may come for love relationships and/or friendships! The point is, people serve different purposes at different times and seasons in our lives, we also serve the same in other people's lives. Consider this analogy: Working in an organisation is like being on a journey, where you either progress and move up the ladder, or face setbacks and leave the organisation. In either case, you never remain stagnant, times and seasons come and go. However, it's important to think about how you want to be treated while you are on this journey. Do you want your colleagues and boss to support you in every challenge and celebrate your victories, or do you prefer being treated poorly?

The same applies if you manage your firm and business. How do you want to be treated on the day of a setback or a victory by colleagues, contemporaries, competitors etc? Now let us translate this analogy into our daily lives. We too are on a journey in life, and there are different levels of growth, times and seasons on this journey, and people who play different roles in these seasons.

How we treat the people who may have completed their season and time in our lives says a lot about our loving status for humans. It also says a lot about how we value ourselves and our expectations of how we want to be treated by others. Because if we profess to be believers, I mean if we truly follow the word of God then we must be giving to people what we want in return right? Give and it shall come back to you (we keep assuming it is just financial, no please it is in all things) ...give love and it comes back, give joy and it comes back to you.... give pain and guess what? Yes, you guessed right, it comes right back at you!

CHAPTER 9

WATCH OUT (A THREE-IN-ONE STORY)

Over the years I have come to appreciate that you have to be careful when dealing with domestic helps: nannies, houseboys and employees like secretaries etc.

The first story I'd like to share has to do with a young man my husband did a pro-bono case for. He had been arrested and prosecuted for stealing. Unfortunately, he didn't have a lawyer. My husband had a case in the same court, had sympathy for him and decided to defend him. One day I followed my husband to court and met this young boy. He looked very miserable, so I decided to mentor him. I am sure you are thinking what kind of crazy decision is that! Yes, that is what I decided to do.

I took his contact and when my husband and I returned to the office, I had my office manager contact him. When he came to see me and told me his life story I arranged for him to go through deliverance at my church, Action Chapel International.

For the next couple of years, anytime he needed money he

would call and I would give it to him. He mainly needed money for school fees for his children. After a while I realized it didn't make any sense to always provide for him when he wasn't working. I needed an ironing boy, so I had him come home and work over the weekends. Gradually he kept staying over for one domestic assignment after the other and eventually, he moved in to stay with us. He was very hardworking, and he stayed with us for four years.

In the fourth year of his stay, my husband started complaining about his monies getting missing and he would always accuse the young man. This would irritate me, and I kept on telling my husband that the fact that the young man was a thief when we met him didn't mean that he was still a thief. However, each time he complained and said he was sure it was the young man who was stealing from him.

One day I sent him on an assignment with a new driver I had employed and when they returned the driver narrated a story to me about how the young man had arranged with a fuel attendant to swindle me out of the money I had provided them for fuel. In fact, I was very upset. When he got back from the assignment I sacked him.

A few months after I sacked him, we realized that money kept getting missing from the house, which didn't make any sense. My husband was sure someone was stealing his money again! We decided to playback the footage of our CCTV cameras and that was when we found that this young man we had sacked had been coming into our home at night between 12 am and 2 am to steal from us. Of course he had lived with us for years, so the dogs knew him and didn't bark at him when he came into the house.

My husband arranged with the very same police officer who arrested him four years prior, to arrest him. We intended to prosecute him, however, he looked so miserable that we considered his children and decided not to pursue the matter.

A few months later, one of the male helpers in the house informed me that this same young man had reached out to him to ask me to forgive him for what he did and that he had lost his firstborn child. Furthermore, everywhere he went to look for work he was turned down.

According to him, he decided to pray about his woes, moving from one prayer camp to another. But, everywhere he went he was informed that he had offended someone who had been good to him, so he should go and seek forgiveness and plead with the person. When I was told this, I agreed to meet with him and asked him to come and see me. He came over and asked for forgiveness and I forgave him.

The second story under this theme has to do with one of my nannies who was very good with the children. However, she developed an attitude and I had to let her go. After she left, she reached out to Kwame, whom I called my chief of staff because he was the domestic staff who had stayed with me the longest. She asked Kwame to plead with me to allow her to come around and sweep in the mornings. I agreed and she returned to work with us, but not as a nanny this time.

Approximately three months after she came back I noticed that she didn't look well, apparently, she had taken seed. After a few months she couldn't work anymore. However, because she had recently come back into our home, my husband and I took responsibility of the pregnancy. We ensured that she had a safe delivery and took care of all her bills. Interestingly, she had a boy and named him Emmanuel after my husband. My children refer to Emmanuel as their cousin.

The third story is about an office manager I had. She was so efficient that she no longer played roles in the office alone but in the home as well, she became a big sister to my kids.

This lady used to have so many dreams centred around relationships. One day she confided in me that she was having recurring dreams where she would come and introduce a man she intended to marry and I would object to it.

A few days later, I received a revelation about the dreams: Her mother had had ten children with three different men. The Holy Spirit ministered to me that the reason why she kept seeing me in her dreams and I would reject the men she brought was because He the Lord had brought her under my wings to help her. I was to ensure that she would not go the way of her mother; to have children with different men but marry and have children with her husband only.

I shared the revelation with her. Apparently, she was not happy and told one of my other employees that she thought if she didn't leave my employ, she would not marry and have children. I was so upset when I heard that, I called her and I told her I didn't want to be the reason why she wouldn't have children or marry so she should leave the organisation.

Just three months after she left, she was impregnated by someone and gave birth out of wedlock, exactly what the Holy Spirit had brought her around me to prevent. She eventually had the baby and had to relocate from Ghana to live with her mother who lived outside the country.

Subsequently one of her sisters came to see me to beg on her behalf. I had no clue what had happened, so I was perplexed. That was when the sister told me that this lady had developed a terrible skin problem. She said they had been to several hospitals with no results. Of course, typical of us Africans, they resorted to prayer. They kept moving from one prayer camp to another, one prayer meeting to another. Apparently everywhere she went she was told that she had offended someone who had been very good to her so she should go and plead. Unfortunately, she felt too proud to come and plead, so her sisters kept coming one after the other over the years so that I would forgive her.

I forgave her eventually and removed her from account in my heart. Seven years after she had left my organisation, I invited her to the birthday party of one of my children and we have since been in constant touch with each other.

Why do I share these three stories? I share these three stories for only one reason.

It is amazing how domestic staff and people who work so closely with us can cause us to sin. I was so upset with these three people that I am sure I said something that became a curse in their lives.

One day the Holy Spirit ministered to me and I realized that I was actually gloating in their pain and their suffering. I had even quoted scripture to support my gloating *"Do not touch my anointed ones and do my prophets no harm"* Psalms 105:15. But then, is that what Jesus would have done in such a situation?

My dear reader, it is very important to watch out where domestic staff and employees are concerned. Because they work in close proximity to us it is very easy for them to offend us and it is very easy for us to hold them to account in our hearts.

By the Grace of God, I know I have released all these three people from account in my heart, and I bear them no grudges. However, I decided to share these stories to help someone else.

Is there a domestic staff who has offended you? A houseboy, a nanny, a gardener, a secretary, a clerk, a security guard? Is it possible you are holding someone in this category to account in your heart? Let it go! Set them free and set your soul free. Guard your heart and ban the enemy from accessing your life.

Food for thought
Hmm

Let us reflect on this! Are you the offender or the offended? We cannot justify our ways with human wisdom. Do you see that we can even search the Bible to support offences? We often face complex situations and decision-making processes that require wisdom and guidance.

While there are a variety of sources we can turn to for insight, the most powerful and transformative way to approach these challenges is by asking ourselves, "What would Jesus do in this instance?" By contemplating this question, we can tap into the ultimate wisdom of God and gain clarity.

I remember a few years ago people had wristbands with WWJD - What Would Jesus Do? - inscribed on them. I don't see those bands around anymore, but the question of WWJD? shouldn't die out as a fashion trend. Let us revive it, not as fashion but as a lifestyle! Not just for the hard tough questions, but for all the things that we do. You may be saying "But I don't know what Jesus would do," please read the word of God and ask the Holy Spirit for guidance, He will lead you in all wisdom.

Or you may say Jesus didn't have the problem I have now, He "lived" when life was simple. News flash! Jesus is still alive; He arose from the dead and He knows all we are going through right now!

Asking WWJD isn't literally saying Jesus has gone through your actual trial e.g. Just because we do not have records of Jesus being sick, doesn't mean we cannot ask the question of WWJD when we are sick. When we ask WWJD, I believe what we are doing is asking Jesus into the situation and seeing the situation through the eyes of Jesus Christ. It means you are giving your situation a Christ perspective, and you are ready to surrender it all to Christ!

However, it is not enough to simply ask the question and hope for the best. To truly benefit from this approach, we must also take the step of obedience. This means being willing to act on the guidance we receive, even if it requires us to make difficult choices or step outside of our comfort zones.

P.S. I strongly believe, and I have learnt that if you are looking at building your prayer life up and becoming more attentive to the promptings of the Holy Spirit, this is the best question to ask yourself on every issue, every time, no matter the decision you have to make, no matter what, even to the choice of clothes to wear, the food to eat, and when to eat it, try it, it works.

CHAPTER 10

OFFENCE IN THE SIGHT OF GOD

I started having a particular problem in the year 2013. This problem gradually became a major prayer point. Sometime in the year 2019, I was praying in the middle of the night when the Holy Spirit told me to go and discuss this problem with my spiritual father, Archbishop Nicholas Duncan Williams[25] (Papa). The next morning I called Papa and asked to see him and he booked me for an afternoon meeting. When I got there, I carefully discussed the problem, went into minute details, told him what I had done about the problem, and the prayer points I had prayed about the issue.

After I had finished talking, he calmly said *'Go, you can handle it, you don't even know what you carry.'* I was taken aback. I sat there looking at him, and he could tell I was surprised by his response. Undoubtedly, I thought he was going to pray for me or give me some advice, but he was not moved and he repeated *'Go, you can handle it, you don't even know what you carry.'* I left his office very confused and dejected. For the

---

25 *Archbishop Nicholas Duncan-Williams is a Ghanaian religious leader and charismatic preacher, serving as the presiding Archbishop and General Overseer of the Action Chapel International Ministry, Headquartered in Accra, Ghana*

next few years every time I prayed about the issue, I would wonder and say *'What I carry, what I carry?' 'Ah this man, didn't he hear what I said, what does he mean by what I carry? If I was carrying something, would I be going through this issue?'*

During Impact[26] 2023, one of the special guests was Apostle Joshua Selman[27]. During one of the morning sessions, after he had finished ministering, Archbishop took over and led us in prayers. Just when he started, the Holy Spirit said *'After impact go and confess to Papa.'* He drew my attention and reminded me of the day I went to discuss the issue with him. He said, *'When you told Papa about the problem and he said 'go, you can handle it, you don't even know what you carry,' you were offended. For the last four years every now and then when you remember the conversation you repeat the statement to yourself.* He continued *'You didn't even realise that Archbishop was giving you a prophetic word because you were so consumed with the burden of the issue. You thought I asked you to discuss the issue so he would pray for you, you missed the prophetic word he gave you.'* Then He said, *'The issue hasn't gone away, yet in two years you have written three books and you have had two translated into French. Do you now understand what he meant by 'go, you can handle it, you don't even know what you carry?'* I was very surprised!

The very next day I called Papa and asked to see him. When I met him, I asked him if he could remember the time when I shared a problem with him and he told me to go and that

---

26 *Impact is an annual convention of Action Chapel International, featuring a host of speakers from across the globe.*
27 *Apostle Joshua Selman is a Nigerian Gospel minister, conference speaker, and televangelist. He is the founder of Koinonia -Eternity Network International.*

I could handle it. Interestingly he remembered, and I said to him that I was not very happy at all at that incident and that every time I remembered I would ask myself *'What I carry, what do I carry?' 'What do I carry?' 'If I carried something, would I be facing this issue?'*

His reaction surprised me. He burst into laughter and then said *"Now lift up your hands and let me pray for you,"* and he prayed for me.

The reason why I am sharing this story is that I didn't even know I was offended by what he said. I thought I was disappointed, and I kept asking myself why he didn't pray for me. But my dear reader, in the eyes of God I was offended and He wanted me to rid my heart of that offence. As a loving Father, He made me go to the Archbishop after four years so I could release him from the judgment in my heart. Glory to Jesus.

Food for thought
Let's pause here and say a quick prayer.

Dear Lord,
I thank you for this testimony.
Please remind me of every offence I hold in my heart.
Lord, please give me rest where my heart is troubled with offence and recall every act of offence disguised in worldly wisdom.
Forgive me and help me forgive, show me how to love your children and see them as you regard them.
Create in me a clean heart and make me always walk in Your love. In Jesus' Name!
Amen!

Why did I ask us to pray? It is because we cannot depend on our memories and that's a fearful truth we need to be aware of. The all-wise Spirit of God is the only 'memory' we can ever depend on. When we are on this journey to release all offences from our hearts, the Holy Spirit will remind us of every past deed and point out every present act that can lead to offence and iniquity. A simple prayer like the one above will unlock many truths, it is not in the wording and eloquence, but it is in the sovereignty of Whom we have trusted with our request.

CHAPTER 11

WHAT A TEST!

In March 2024, one of the Full Gospel chapters contacted me and asked me to speak at their weekly chapter meeting. The topic the Holy Spirit gave me was *'Heart cleansing, a Catalyst for Revival.'* However, the Holy Spirit told me that the members of the chapter had to ensure they had at least twenty people who had read my book *An Available Vessel for the Lord's Pleasure* present on the day I would speak.

For some reason any time I would pray into the meeting, I would sense discomfort. I really felt I was not to speak at the chapter, but I could not put a finger on the reason. As a result of the discomfort I told one of my mentees to prepare on the same topic so that just in case the Holy Spirit didn't give me a release to speak, the chapter would not be without a speaker.

This discomfort persisted for close to a month and on the D-day, even as I drove to the meeting, I still had the discomfort. When I got to the meeting and I was introduced as the speaker, I asked how many people had read the book and only two people showed their hands. I then told them that one of the things I am keen on is obeying the voice of the Holy Spirit, and He had told me that I should ensure that at least twenty people had read the book before I spoke. I continued and said that since at least twenty people had not read the book, I would not be speaking.

However, I introduced my mentee to speak. She had prepared certain scriptures to lead them in prayer so I told them that maybe as my mentee led, the Holy Spirit would indicate to me what the whole thing was about. I sat and she started leading the prayer. About seven minutes into the prayer, I got it! The Holy Spirit said, *'It is a test, it is a test, it is a test,'* so I signalled her, and ended the prayer session. The Holy Spirit started ministering to me and said to tell them that it was a test. And that they had come to listen to a talk on heart cleansing as a catalyst for revival yet when I said I couldn't speak and asked my mentee Victoria to speak, most of them were offended and some of them were murmuring and complaining, saying they didn't come to listen to Victoria, they came to listen to me. They had not even obeyed the straightforward and simple instruction to read the book before the meeting. They were sitting there in disobedience, yet they wanted to receive from the Lord!

Then the Holy Spirit drew my attention that one person actually got up and walked out of the room when Victoria started the prayer session. He said it was just a test, their hearts were so dense and not ready for revival. Even though they were coming for a meeting on heart cleansing, their attitude was wrong. That was the test the Holy Spirit administered. They had the wrong posture and attitude, there is no way that He was going to talk to them or do anything for them that day.

My dear, it was very clear that their hearts were far from the meeting. It also became very clear that they had just wanted to tick a box that they had had a speaker for that occasion and not that they were ready to receive from the speaker.

I learnt a lot from that experience and it made me more resolute to obey the voice of the Holy Spirit, especially when it didn't make sense in the least, like in this case.

Food for thought
Are we ready for the REVIVAL we keep asking for?
We keep seeking a revival in the church, calling for the Azusa Street and the days of Elijah! Ooooh-but are we ready? Can we walk in total obedience and submission? Can we promptly obey the 'Nonsense' directions and not seek to make 'sense' of the Holy Spirit, using our feeble minds to understand God?

Can we carry the move of the Holy Spirit without bending to the pressures of the world? Let us truthfully ponder on this for a moment: can we confidently say we are positioned for a revival? These are some hard questions I ask myself, to keep myself from letting my emotions lead the way, instead of being guided by the Truth. I came into this knowledge not long ago. I have come to understand that revival starts from the individual and then affects a group, a community, a town, a nation and then the world! Have you wondered why on the day of Pentecost the tongues of fire settled on individuals in the upper room and not on them as a group? You see it wasn't described as a cloud of fire that surrounded and swallowed them up. It was an "individual tongues of fire affair." It has always been an individual process and still is.

May we stop looking at others to bring us a revival. May we cleanse ourselves and our hearts in our inner room and be empowered to affect lives and bear fruits. "When the Day of Pentecost had fully come, they were all with one accord in one place. And suddenly there came a sound from heaven, as of a rushing mighty wind, and it filled the whole house where they were sitting. ***Then there appeared to them divided tongues, as of fire, and one sat upon each of them.*** *And they were all filled with the Holy Spirit and began to speak with other tongues, as the Spirit gave them utterance." **Acts 2:1-4***

CHAPTER 12

THE CANCER OF PRIDE AND EGO

In April 2024, I came across a video where my spiritual father Archbishop Nicholas Duncan Williams was talking about an issue that he had had with his spiritual father, Archbishop Benson Idahosa[28]. In the said video, Archbishop Duncan Williams tells a story about a time when he held a very powerful crusade in Ghana, several years ago.

This crusade was later reported in an Oral Roberts[29] Ministry bulletin, indicating that his church, the Action Faith Ministry was a branch of Archbishop Idahosa's church. This didn't go down well with Archbishop Duncan Williams, and he wrote to the Oral Roberts Ministry requesting that the article be retracted and edited to indicate that his church was not a branch of Archbishop Idahosa's Church. Oral Roberts sent a copy of the letter to Archbishop Idahosa, who then sent a letter to Archbishop Nicholas Duncan Williams

---

[28] *Archbishop Benson Idahosa (1938-1998) was a charismatic Pentecostal preacher who founded the Church of God Mission International. He is widely known as the father of Pentecostalism in Nigeria. Idahosa also founded Benson Idahosa University in Benin City, Edo State, Nigeria.*
[29] *Oral Roberts (1918-2009) was an American Charismatic Christian televangelist.*

requesting for him to come to Benin State to meet with him. Archbishop Duncan Williams refused to honour the invitation. Even when a two-man delegation was sent to him, he refused to honour the invitation. Archbishop Idahosa then wrote to him indicating that *'since he had shown that he had come of age he was now on his own!'* Archbishop Duncan Williams recounts that he tore up the letter and burnt it with a prideful heart.

According to the Archbishop, the years that followed after that incident were terrible for him. It was as though the heavens were closed and everything that could go wrong went wrong. He was besieged and attacked with one problem after the other, it didn't matter how much he prayed, nothing happened.

After much prayer and intercession, he was led to a senior Pentecostal minister who after praying and seeking the face of God informed him that the Lord said he had offended one of His anointed, referring to the issue between him and his spiritual father Archbishop Idahosa. He eventually swallowed his pride and ego and went to seek forgiveness from his spiritual father. When he apologized, Archbishop Idahosa forgave him and accepted his apology. Then Archbishop Idahosa addressed the enemy and said, *"Satan this is a problem between my spiritual son and I, stay out of it!"*

I learnt a few things from this short story. First, I learnt the humility of Archbishop Duncan Williams. The fact that he would tell this story in public and say that the way he behaved was as a result of pride and ego, and that at the time he thought he had 'arrived' because he was the biggest name in the country as there were no other charismatic churches in Ghana.

The second thing I learnt from this story was the fact that even though he was a very powerful spiritual man, according to him it looked as if the heavens were closed during the period he had offended his spiritual father. It didn't matter how much he prayed; nothing was happening.

It stands to reason that you could offend someone, and the Lord would refuse to hear your prayer. This brings to mind Psalm 66:18 which reads, *"if I regard iniquity in my heart the Lord will not hear me."*

These are two important lessons I learnt from that story and I thought it was important to share… sharing is caring.

What have you learnt from the story?

Food for thought
When you subject yourself to spiritual mentorship you must realize the responsibilities it comes with!

The lessons from this video are profound especially as you hear Archbishop Duncan williams himself talk of how iniquity brought him down and caused him pain in his life. I learnt three things:

1. It hammers on the fact and reality, that it is not enough to just join in the chorus of calling a preacher or spiritually revered person 'Mummy' and 'Papa!' Those titles come with responsibility, a heavy responsibility, both from the mentor and the mentee. But above all, we need to realize that heaven recognises the roles we have assigned the person and we have taken on.

We have to be careful who we subject ourselves to, to be an authority over us, because we do not know the covenant the person has with God, and also, mainly because God will defend His own, He fights for His own.

2. Offense may easily cause us to disrespect an individual and the authority they hold over us. Whilst you may see their humanity and their flaws because you are close to them, God sees their heart and sacrifice.

Please let us reflect on the life of King David in the Bible. God saw his heart and preserved him. Even though he may have been considered a sexually flawed and immoral personality, God preserved his house and made it no secret that David's heart *pleased Him. (please see the life and relationship between David and God in 1 and 2 Samuel, please add the Psalms written by David to the reading list).*

3. *Yes, indeed the Archbishop was also anointed, but it became obvious that there are levels of sacrifices and God is ultimately a Just God who honours covenants! Oh, such a wonderful and fearful thing to know that God fights for His own, and fearful to be on the other side filled with pride such that God Himself resists you.*

Psalms 138:6:
"Though the Lord is on high,
Yet He regards the lowly;
But the proud He knows from afar".

James 4:6:
"But He gives more grace. Therefore, He says:
"God resists the proud,
But gives grace to the humble".

Above all, I pray we do not overlook the spiritual greatness that the Holy Spirit has bestowed upon an individual during their lifetime. Rather than waiting until after their passing, we should take the time to recognize and appreciate their anointing while they are still with us. We must honour and respect this anointing that enriches our spiritual journey, so we can continue to grow and develop!

Please let us Give honour now!

CHAPTER 13

FOOD

In January 2024, the Holy Spirit impressed on me to gather a group of ladies for a half-day retreat to talk about how to guard the heart and how to identify the little things that block our hearts and prevent God from hearing us and anything associated with that.

A few of the group leaders and I started praying into the meeting. As we prayed, the Holy Spirit started giving me a few revelations into the meeting.

There was one particular revelation that took me off guard. One of the days as I prayed into the meeting I heard *'FOOD.'* I said *"FOOD?"* and He repeated *"FOOD."* He said, *'You like to quote my body is the temple of God, yet you treat my temple as a rubbish dump. You don't pay attention to what you put in the body and when you finish you turn around and pray for good health. Watch the food you eat, watch what you throw into the body, stop treating the temple of God as a rubbish dump.'*

Have you ever thought about your body and the food you eat in this manner? I surely had never thought about that! It was a big eye-opener. The Holy Spirit started by saying *'It is your body, but it is My temple.'* Then He went on to talk about the fact that any time we quote: *"the body is the temple of God"* (1Corinthians 3:16-17) we relate it to sexual immorality, but He wanted to draw our attention to food.

This is one of the ways the enemy gets access to our health: the way we treat our body, His temple. We should be mindful of what we put in our bodies.

If we won't just throw anything at all in our bedrooms and on our beds, we shouldn't put just anything into His temple. He drew my attention to heart disease. Cleansing of the heart includes cleansing the heart of grease and anything that clogs it through the kinds of food we subject our organs to. The organs are in His temple, and overworking the organs is abusing His temple.

Could you please pay attention to what you put in your body? Please don't treat your body, the temple of God as a rubbish dump!

Food for thought

A couple of months ago the Holy Spirit, through my mentor Auntie Kuukua instructed me to have my medicals done. I got straight into it, doing a host of tests. One day, whilst in conversation with the Holy Spirit about the medicals I was undergoing He ministered to me. He reminded me of the time Christ said '... when the enemy came, he found nothing in Me! (John 14:30)' And He said, nothing may be found in you spiritually, but something may be found in your physical structure (the body) which houses the Spirit! He said I must see to the total package and not focus on just maintaining the Spirit! Wow! I had not considered that; I was busy concentrating on "keeping" a clean heart and not paying much attention to my physical body and its condition.

I started reflecting on how over the years I would wonder how young people serving God with such dedication would die from things like organ failure, obesity, and some stress-related conditions. I had questions that boggled my mind about how these things could happen to people who were so dedicated to God and Kingdom service. Just recently I have been led to the answer to my musings in Proverbs 4:23 'Keep your heart with all diligence, for out of it spring the issues of life.'

You see the word in that scripture charges us to do the keeping, not any other person's responsibility but our own individual responsibility. That means the same diligence with which we keep our (spiritual)hearts, must be the same which ensures that nothing is found in our physical bodies when the enemy comes with sickness and disease. It is our very own responsibility.

Let us perform an introspection. Is our 'housing/ temple' in good shape? If we cannot answer that question confidently with medical facts and reports then we need to start cleaning now!!

Please, are you ignoring a pain, a discomfort you feel in your body? Are you exercising regularly? Are you drinking enough water?

Do you know the state of your heart and all other organs? Let us boldly rebuke any fear that prevents us from seeking medical attention. We should not let the lack of knowledge rob us of our lives! Let us indeed be able to declare the words of Christ in John 14:30 "I will no longer talk much with you, for the ruler of this world is coming, **and he has nothing in Me!**" Amen.

REFLECTION

From the various short stories shared in Part One, I hope it has become abundantly clear that we have a lot to do as Christians. I have gradually come to appreciate how most of our pressing prayer points are not answered. I am now no longer surprised to see many people spend several years binding and losing, blocking spiritual attacks, and dealing with background and bloodline issues, yet nothing seems to be happening.

Could it be that most of the problems we have as Christians are of our own making? Could it be that we are quick to blame witches and demons for our problems without first checking the condition of our hearts? In Psalm 66:18, the Bible says that, 'if we regard iniquity in our hearts, the Lord will not hear us. Is it possible the Lord doesn't hear us most of the time because of iniquities in our hearts: pride, arrogance, self-righteousness, anger, bitterness, pain, offences, and the list goes on?

Before you go to the next chapter of this book, may I humbly ask you to pause and reflect on the condition of your heart?

Could you go a step further and release anyone you are holding to account in your heart due to offence, pain, anger, and/or pride?

May the Lord bless you and keep you. May He cause His face to shine upon you and grant you the peace that passes all understanding. Amen.

PART TWO

CHAPTER PRELUDE

In this part of the book, I will be sharing a few of the meetings that I have held over the last year on the topics regarding the heart. In this part, we will also be reading a few of the testimonies of people who were part of the meetings.

They will be sharing the effect the topic had on them and what they did after the meetings.

CHAPTER 14

HOPE DEFERRED MAKES THE HEART SICK

In June 2023, one of the Full Gospel chapters in the Airport municipality[30] in Accra invited me to speak on any topic of my choice. The Holy Spirit asked me to speak on: *'Hope Deferred Makes the Heart Sick.'*

As I pondered over the topic and went before the Lord to pray and ask what exactly to say, the Holy Spirit started teaching me what He would want me to teach His people at the meeting. He started by ministering to me that there is so much prayer going on yet there is so much disappointment in the body of Christ, and most of His children were suffering because of hope deferred. However, many of them don't realize that their hope is deferred because their prayers are not answered, and their prayers are not answered because of the state of their hearts.

He said that there are so many people living with a lot of offence and anger in their hearts, thus when they pray,

---

30 *Airport Residential Area is a suburb in the Accra Metropolitan district, a district of the Greater Accra Region of Ghana.*

He does not hear them, and because of that a lot of the prophecies they hear do not come to pass. He continued ministering, saying that most of the prophecies are right, yet they do not come to pass because the condition of the heart of the recipient is not conducive for the prophecy to take place.

When I got to the meeting and started the ministration, mid-way the Holy Spirit asked me to stop. He ministered that there was someone in the meeting who could relate so well to what I was talking about in the meeting, that person had vowed never to speak to someone again in his life. He told me to ask the person to come out and speak. That is how Sammy came out and broke down in front of everybody and shared his testimony which you are going to read next, enjoy.

Testimonies

I am Samuel and I work with the Ghana Health Service[31] as a driver. I purchased a copy of *An Available Vessel for the Lord's Pleasure* when the book was released. I subsequently asked for ten copies to sell for the author on a trip to Sunyani[32]. I have since been instrumental in delivering free copies of the books to hotel lobbies as directed by Auntie Kuukua, and I have passionately sold copies of the books. I have learnt a host of lessons from reading *An Available Vessel for the Lord's Pleasure*. Although I was a tongues-speaking, and water baptized Christian, my relationship with the Holy Spirit was not strong. However, that has changed, my relationship with the Holy Spirit is growing and I eagerly seek Him. Also, He continuously saves me and delivers me.

One of my most recent encounters with deliverance occurred when I attended a meeting where Aunty Kuukua was scheduled to speak, at Airport View Hotel[33]. She talked about not holding bitterness and grudges towards anyone in your heart, and the hindrances bitterness and grudges cause. She then said that there was someone in the room going through that situation. It was me!

I got up and walked straight to her and started crying. The

---

31 *The Ghana Health Service (GHS) is a Ghanaian government body established in 1996 as part of the Health Sector Reform of Ghana. The Health Service is under the Ministry of Health in Ghana.*

32 *Sunyani is a town in west-central Ghana, it is the capital city of the Bono Region and the Sunyani Municipal of Ghana.*

33 *Airport View Hotel is a 3-star hotel located in the Airport Residential Area suburb of Accra, Ghana. Situated just 5 kilometres from the city centre, with a view of the Kotoka International Airport.*

issue was that I had held my mum's funeral a few weeks prior to attending that meeting and because of some actions my uncle put up after the funeral, I had decided not to have anything to do with him again. I even blocked his number and cautioned my children not to visit him.

I came to that meeting so that I would have the chance to meet Aunty Kuukua after the meeting and tell her this story. Little did I know that the Holy Spirit had already prepared her, but she didn't know that it was me. After the meeting ended, she asked me to call my uncle and check on him. My uncle was on his sickbed. The following day was a holiday, so she told me to go and visit him and not go empty-handed. I had issues with my uncle because of money, yet here she was saying I should go and give him money on top of everything. Sometimes the directions of the Holy Spirit seem very nonsensical, but who are you to challenge the wisdom of the Spirit of God?

I went home and did as I had been instructed and came back relieved! The enemy normally causes hatred between people so that he can capitalise on it to block your blessings from the Lord. We should always try not to hold grudges against each other.

- *Sammy*

My name is Joan, I work as a lawyer with KuukuaA Legal Consulting[34]. Before working as a lawyer, even before passing my bar exams, I had struggled for over a year with law school little did I know it was related to me holding someone to account in my heart. I have known Auntie Kuukua who I affectionately call Mummy since 2022. I was gifted a copy of her book *An Available Vessel for the Lord's Pleasure* by a friend, and I later got in touch with her through a text message, because the book really impacted me. I had always wanted to have a personal relationship with the Holy Spirit, and the book was an answer to my prayer for a deeper walk with the Holy Spirit.

Since 2022 I have grown in my walk with the Holy Spirit. I share my growth testimony in her second book *Did I Bear Fruits?* where I share some of my major takeaways from the book *An Available Vessel for the Lord's Pleasure*[35]. I am a work in progress, and I would like to share one of those major points here. I realise that the Holy Spirit has been on a mission to heal my heart and cleanse me from any darkness in my heart. This started after I read chapter 35 of *An Available Vessel for the Lord's Pleasure* and the process continues.

We had a seminar at the Airport View Hotel in 2023. Mummy was the speaker, and her text was from Psalm 66:18 *"If I regard iniquity in my heart the Lord will not hear me."* She explained that iniquity goes beyond just disobedience

---
34 *KuukuaA Legal Consulting is a legal firm in Airport, Accra Ghana. See Kuukuaalegalconsulting.com.*
35 *'An Available Vessel for the Lord's Pleasure' is the first book of Kuukua Maurice Ankrah, it is a collection of over 60 powerful testimonies which demonstrate the power of the Holy Spirit in the life of a believer.*

to the Holy Spirit because it is an intentional and wilful disobedience. She also explained that Christians spend time praying but don't receive answers due to iniquity and unforgiveness and that everyone in the meeting had one person they were not speaking with so we should take out our phones and unblock that person we had blocked and send a message to the person who had offended us or whom we had offended.

She explained further that, we could be 'right' but the anger we had in our hearts would prevent us from receiving answers to our prayers and it would lead to our hope being deferred and our hearts would be sick

As Mummy spoke, it reminded me of something the Lord had me do. Sometime in 2019, I was praying to the Lord about school admission. I had no idea that the answer to my prayer lay in forgiving someone whom I held to account in my heart. When I did forgive the person, the door opened, and my prayer was answered. He again reminded me that I had to unblock another person so right at the seminar meeting, I unblocked the other person who had offended me, and I felt so much better. I sent a message to the person. He never responded but since then, I can share the story without feeling the pain. I feel like a burden has been lifted off me.

- Joan

Food for thought

I have been in meetings where Mummy(Auntie Kuukua) has made the declaration to mend bridges as led by the Holy Spirit. She would often ask people gathered at the meetings who would not be speaking to someone or would have blocked people on their phones, or would be holding someone to account in their hearts to immediately pray to release those people from the grudge they bore them in their hearts and then follow through with the action of actually unblocking people from the call list and sending out messages to reach out to the persons. She would ask that they send a message saying 'Hello' 'Happy New Year' etc, encouraging us to take action and to mend a burnt bridge.

I have been in those meetings and, I would search myself every time and ask myself if I had missed someone and pray that the Holy Spirit would bring the person to mind.

After reading the testimonies in this chapter, and as I type this, I realise I have gone through several testimonies all about the heart and not performed the introspection exercise nor the mending burnt bridges exercise. Now the reason I keep checking over and over again and performing that exercise is because I know that iniquity can disguise itself in things that appear 'okay,' pride can easily set in and self-righteousness can follow and bit by bit, the entire iniquity 'clan' can move and settle in the heart.

That's why I would like us to pause and take a moment and do an introspection. Especially the mending bridges and unblocking exercise. I just realised that there could be someone- probably you- who is reading this right now, still holding a grudge or has anger simmering in their heart.

There is no big or small offence or iniquity. Iniquity is iniquity,

I mean if all we need to move a mountain is a mustard seed of Faith, I am sure all we need to block our prayers is less than a grain of iniquity.

Please join me in taking this action, I am sure by now you already know the person you need to be reaching out to, to fix the problem and liberate your heart. Learning and sharing from what I have experienced sitting under the ministrations of Auntie Kuukua, if there is someone you have blocked on your phone if there's someone you have on your naughty list of who you think to yourself "Oh, I can never forgive,!" please forgive the person.

Is there someone in your inbox whom you have shut off because you have said to yourself, "I can never forgive and I cannot forget, I am not God, I am not cut out for this?" You know all those weird things we say to justify iniquity in our hearts. Could you please take your phone? Just put this book down for a few seconds.

Please scroll through your phone contacts. Find those numbers that you have blocked. Send a hello. Send a quick short message. Let me help you with a few examples you could send out.

1. Happy New Year –If you haven't spoken to the person the whole year, technically it is still the new year.
2. Hello, I thought of you. I hope you are well. Stay blessed.
3. You came to mind, I am just checking in.
4. May you have a blessed day today.
5. I hope we can talk soon. Have a good week.

These are some quick messages I have learnt over the years performing this exercise by following Auntie Kuukua to her speaking engagements. Trust me it is an instant liberation.

Please remember, you are not doing this because you expect a response from the person, but because you are setting your heart free of iniquity. You are taking your name off the 'accuser of the brethren's list.' The enemy cannot accuse you of that offence before God anymore, Glory Hallelujah!

Additionally, please apologise to whoever you need to apologise to. If you did the hurting, please apologise. Take your phone and be strong, and bold. Please apologise to the person you spoke evil about, the person you've turned your back on, someone who was very helpful to you. Apologise now and start the process. Don't wait for that big moment or say I have to go to the house, visit, sit down and all the cultural drama, please do it now. Please pick up your phone and say that apology before you start rationalising and decide against it.

Please pick up your phone and say "I am sorry for all the pain I caused you over the years. I pray you forgive me." Pick up your phone and say to that person, "I hope I get to speak with you so that I can apologise properly." For being ungrateful, pick up the phone and say, "Thank you" to that person you haven't said thank you to. Say, "Thank you for all you've done for me, words cannot express how much I am grateful to you."

Beloved, let's do this right now. Let's not wait. PLEASE don't wait until you finish reading this book. No! Do this right now! Release that person from bondage in your heart. Sometimes all it takes is a simple text message.

Ps. Please type your words out in full. Using shorthand may communicate disrespect.

CHAPTER 15

MY FLESH MY ENEMY

The very first time I spoke at a church gathering was at the Assemblies of God[36] church, Afienya[37]. When I got the invitation, I had to choose a topic and I chose *'My Flesh, My Enemy.'* In preparation for the talk, which was basically going to address how our flesh hinders our prayers, the Holy Spirit gave me Galatians 5:16-21.

> *I say then: Walk in the Spirit, and you shall not fulfil the lust of the flesh. For the flesh lusts against the Spirit, and the Spirit against the flesh; and these are contrary to one another so that you do not do the things that you wish. But if you are led by the Spirit, you are not under the law. Now the works of the flesh are evident, which are: adultery, fornication, uncleanness, lewdness, idolatry, sorcery, hatred, contentions, jealousies, outbursts of wrath, selfish ambitions, dissensions, heresies, envy, murders, drunkenness, revelries, and the like; of which I tell you beforehand, just as I also told you in time past, that those who*

---

[36] The Assemblies of God (AG) is an International Pentecostal denomination. It was founded in Ghana in 1931 by two American missionaries. From humble beginnings, it has now grown to become one of the largest Pentecostal denominations in Ghana.

[37] Afienya is a community on the Akosombo road near Tema in the Greater Accra Region of Ghana.

practice such things will not inherit the kingdom of God. But the fruit of the Spirit is love, joy, peace, longsuffering, kindness, goodness, faithfulness, gentleness, self-control. Against such, there is no law.

He said that most times when this scripture is quoted Christians like to emphasize on fornication and lust, as though those are the only two sins of the flesh; but He wanted me to address anger. Anger? I was a little perplexed because I was already feeling a little uncomfortable about going to speak in a church setting.

Undoubtedly, the Assemblies of God is a very word-versed church, they do know their scriptures. I didn't see how I had to concentrate on only anger as the topic, but I obeyed.

When I got to the church, I told them that the Holy Spirit had sent me to talk to them about anger. The whole room was quiet, all of them stared at me. I said, *'Well, I am just being obedient to the voice of the Holy Spirit, the scripture He gave me is Galatians 5; focusing on verses 19 to 21.'* I said to them that I didn't know why He said I should speak about anger, but I was going to obey and speak about anger.

The Holy Spirit then referred me to Ephesians 4:26 which says, *"Be angry, and do not sin: do not let the sun go down on your wrath."* I explained that we have all sorts of health issues because of pain, bitterness, and anger. I told them that there's a good reason why the Bible says that we should not allow the sun to go down on our anger because God in His wisdom knows what pain, bitterness, offence, and anger do to our health.

I shared a personal experience of how I had blocked someone and my justification for blocking the person was anchored in Matthew 5:30, *"And if your right hand causes you to sin, cut it off and cast it from you; for it is more profitable for you that one of your members perish, than for your whole body to be cast into hell."*

I also shared how the Holy Spirit had led me to unblock the person and led me to send a message to the person. I shared the revelation that the Holy Spirit had given me on the scripture and how many believers had wrongly used the scripture to justify their anger.

As I was talking, the Holy Spirit stopped me and said to me that there were three people there who could testify to what I was saying. He told me to invite those three people to come up before I could continue.

That is when a gentleman got up and started crying. It was unbelievable. Usually, it is accepted that women are emotional, and cry easily in such settings, but to see an elderly man get up and start crying was something else. This man came forward and shared a story about him and his younger brother. In fact, in that meeting, I cried, and so did many of the congregants. The atmosphere was infused with pain, it was emotionally charged!

Some of the people in the meeting had to forgive their teachers; a woman shared her story of how she had been angry with her teacher from her old school. Bill and his wife both shared a story about a problem that existed between him and his younger brother.

A woman shared her story of how she and her husband were not in a good place and how she had planned not to forgive her husband. A man also shared the story of the fracas between him and his son who now lived in the US. He recounted how he had spent his resources to educate his son and how his son had now refused to take care of him. He had vowed not to have anything to do with his son anymore.

As he shared his story, I ministered to him and asked him to get in touch with his son. By the leading of the Holy Spirit, I perceived that the relationship between the man and his son must be repaired. I was reminded of Exodus 20:12, *"Honor your father and your mother, that your days may be long upon the land which the Lord your God is giving you."* The path that his son had taken was a dangerous path that could cut short his life. Unfortunately, all calls to the son went unanswered.

The stories that follow are testimonies from two of the people who were in that meeting. They have shared the impact that meeting had on their lives.

Testimonies

I connected closely with the testimony of another testifier, Bill. Bill is my husband and he had challenges with his siblings. These are siblings that we had lived with in Singapore. What they did to him, although not directed at me, affected me because of how it affected my husband. I felt they could have shown him more respect, and they caused problems between my in-laws and I.

Initially, it was really hard to let go, but I knew that somehow God did it for our good. Nevertheless, whenever the issue came up, I would see Bill's pain, and I would tell him to let it go. When I saw him go to the altar when Kuukua spoke, I knew the Holy Spirit was working on him. He has since been very light in Spirit.

For me, it was easy to let go of grudges against the people who had hurt me because most of them were dead. I reflected on this as Kuukua spoke that day. I recalled people from my childhood who had verbally abused me, words that hurt and would follow me through life and affect my self-worth. As I reflected on those, I set them free in my heart because it is quite easy to let go if one understands the fact that sometimes God allows things to happen to build us up. After all, He is available to help us go through them.

That meeting helped me because at my workplace I faced racism, yet I did not allow anyone to imprison me with their actions. I did not hold them to account in my heart. Because of that, there was no rancour or bitterness, and I was free. I thank God for the power of the Holy Spirit in me and how

He keeps helping me go through it all. It is a great journey.

I believe this is the preaching that people need to hear, the prosperity teaching is becoming too much. We need to hear these kinds of messages. As ambassadors of Christ, we need to reconcile the world to God, and if we cannot let go of hurts, and continue to bear grudges, then how do we play the peacekeeping role for the world?

- Akua Agyemang

For several years I thought I had forgiven my brother who had hurt me. For a very long time, I felt betrayed and unappreciated by him. I noticed it was affecting our relationship because he was drifting away from me. I thought it was fine. I was waiting for him to come and apologize first.

After the engagement with Kuukua, I gathered the courage to simply let go. I made the move towards reconciliation with my younger brother. Since then I've gotten him a job and for the first time in many years, he looks happy. Letting go of hurt is not easy but it's the right thing to do.

- Bill

Food for thought

This Sunday my children learnt in Sunday school that "there is consciousness in heaven." We continued the conversation in the car on our way home. I asked them to explain what it meant to say there is consciousness in heaven. I asked them what is consciousness? It went round and around, but they finally got to the answer and said "It means being aware, and not being unaware." Now that's simple and true. I asked them what is meant when it is said that "there is consciousness in heaven and in hell as well." They spoke about how in hell people would feel the pain of the fire and everything, and in heaven you will feel the peace, the joy, the laughter. In other words, we will be aware of everything in heaven. They then made the connection with the bible story of Lazarus and the rich man. How Lazarus ended up in Abraham's bosom and the rich man ended up in hell. The rich man was so tortured and thirsty that he wanted a drop of water.

I truly enjoyed listening to them. So, what is the connection between my Sunday school lesson from my children and the testimonies we just read? The connection is consciousness.

My major takeaway from both the testimonies and the Sunday school class my children gave me is that, it's not a bad thing to be conscious, we are created to be conscious of ourselves.

I learnt that it is not a bad thing to be conscious of the things that happen to us. The pain we feel, the betrayal, the joy, peace, love, everything. I believe it is good we were created to have this consciousness. I have also grown to believe that one of the main reasons why we have this consciousness is to learn and to make the forgiveness journey more meaningful. Every time our consciousness is released from pain and hurt we know we're making some progress.

Yet if we didn't have this consciousness, we would not know that our heart is in a healing process or has been healed.

Don't despise the pain you feel when hurt, it is the checker that you need to get to work ASAP to rid yourself of any ensuing damage the hurt may bring with it.

We should also be conscious of the fact that the Holy Spirit takes away pain. We are not ruled by pain. We must feel pain and we must equally feel the joy when the pain is no longer there. We must be conscious of all these emotions given by God.

Feel the joy of the Lord, knowing it can replace that pain. Amen

CHAPTER 16

HEART CLEANSING (1)

In February 2024, I was invited to speak at IGEM[38] (International Glorious Eagle Ministries). The Holy Spirit asked that I speak on the topic *'Heart cleansing: A catalyst for revival.'* This is a relatively small budding fellowship and the members had read my book *An Available Vessel for the Lord's Pleasure*. Before the meeting, the Holy Spirit asked members of the fellowship to read the scriptures Psalm 51:10-12, Psalm 24:3-4, Proverbs 4:23 and Psalms 66:18, in preparation for the meeting.

As with previous meetings, the Holy Spirit led me to tell the members to unblock anyone they had blocked on their contact list, due to anger and unforgiveness.

My mission that day was on pain and bitterness and how they hinder the prayers of Christians. Using my testimonies, I shared a lesson the Holy Spirit had taught me recently in relation to my mother. He taught me that my siblings and I should be careful how we treated our mother and this is

---

38 *International Glorious Eagle Ministries (IGEM) is a non-denominational 'after service' fellowship located in Tse-Addo, a suburb of Teshie in Accra Ghana.*

because we had been a little frustrated with her lately. The Holy Spirit pointed out to me that in our frustration, we could be moved by the enemy to disrespect her.

The Holy Spirit reminded me and to remind my siblings that we are all where we are today as a result of our Mother's prayers. He said because she worked as a librarian, she had enough time on her hands to devote to prayer and training us and that is what has made all of us successful in life and in our Christian walk.

The following testimonies are from two people who were in that meeting.

Testimonies

An Available Vessel for the Lord's Pleasure is one of the first books I read this year. As I read the book, the testimony on penance had the most impact on me.

A few weeks after I finished reading the book, I was informed by my pastor that we would have a meeting with Mrs. Kuukua. I had some questions on some parts of the book I had read; I was eager to ask her.

When she came to the programme she spoke about our hearts, the people we hold to account in our hearts, and the need to forgive them in order to move on. I wasn't on good terms with my father, I had never been on good terms with my father, our relationship was very poor and strained. That day I prayed about my father's issue, asking God to help me understand him and to let all the bitterness go.

I never had fatherly love growing up, I met my father for the first time when my mom died in 2015, I was fifteen years old. Several family members had shared what they knew about my conception. In a pretty messed up situation, my mother had me with her aunt's husband.

The following Sunday after the program, as I was getting ready for church, I took a short nap and saw a vision of everything that had happened before I was born. I saw how my mom lived and grew up with my father and her aunt. I saw the affair that led to my conception and how my mom was eventually maltreated after she had me, causing her to leave the house and change my name.

In this revelation, I realized it wasn't entirely my dad's fault, but the family had also prevented him from taking responsibility of me. After I woke up from having that revelation, I noticed that all the pain and anger I had had towards my father was gone. I felt at peace. I am grateful to God that Mrs. Kuukua wrote that book.

- Esinam

My name is Mawuvi, I work as a paralegal at KuukuaA Legal Consulting. I first met Madame Kuukua in 2021 and it was a life-changing encounter. I share this encounter in detail in Chapter 59 of *An Available Vessel for the Lord's Pleasure:'A stepping stone to Victory.'* Nevertheless, I would summarize it here to give context to my growth and the testimony I am about to share.

I was born into a Christian home and I have served in the church since I was a little boy. My parents got divorced when I was a teenager and I had to live with my pastor in his home. My service in the church continued and grew into a 'religious' activity. At best, I was only going through a routine.

I couldn't hold a job, my emotions were all over the place, and I became suicidal when my love relationship fell apart. This was my life at the time I attended an interview with Madame Kuukua in 2021. Little did I know that the Holy Spirit had gone ahead to prepare a place for me in her firm and created a new path for me. My role since then has evolved. I am not just an employee but also a member of the Meet the Author Series team. The Holy Spirit is not done with me,

He continues to heal me. In this testimony, I share how the Holy Spirit through Madame Kuukua's ministry healed my heart.

On the 25th day of February 2024, the MTA team accompanied Madame for a meeting at International Glorious Eagle Ministries (IGEM). She spoke on the topic *'Heart Cleansing: A Catalyst For Revival.'* She ministered about unforgiveness and its impact on our hearts; the power that unforgiveness wields against the spiritual growth of a Christian.

At the time my mother and father got married, my father already had three children: two girls and a boy. My mother also had a baby boy from a previous relationship, during the subsistence of their marriage, I was born.

My parents also adopted some of our external family members who all lived with us. Throughout my childhood, we all lived together as one big family until my parents separated. After the separation, I relocated to my pastor's house to further my education.

This separation caused a gradual decay in the relationship I had had with my family, to the extent that for over a decade, I lost complete touch with my siblings and my birth parents. The bond we had had as a family was broken because everyone had gone their separate ways after the separation. Some of the family members nursed bitterness in their hearts against each other. My father didn't want anything to do with my mother and the children, and I always found myself in the middle feeling angry, hurt, and sad.

I adapted my life by getting close to and attaching myself to people who treated me as family. These included my Pastor and his family and some of my schoolmates. When it came to my blood family, I had to take practical and intentional steps to always communicate or check up on them.

As I was sitting in the meeting at IGEM the Holy Spirit started ministering to me about my blood family. The Holy Spirit told me that one of the things that had been holding me back recently had been the unforgiveness, hurt and pain I felt towards my family and that even though I had been taking practical and intentional steps to communicate with them, I had not fully forgiven them.

At that point, I knew I had to let them go from my heart and cleanse my heart of all rancour. I decided to get in touch with every one of them so I created a WhatsApp page and called it "HOME." I was able to get all my siblings together on one platform and in one place for the first time in over fifteen years.

On this 'Home' page, we took turns to share and update each other about what was going on with us individually and shared fond memories of growing up together. Today the page is active, and we are checking up and keeping in touch with each other almost every day.

My family has been reunited because the Holy Spirit through Madame taught me about cleansing my heart and the effects subtle and "hidden" unforgiveness can have on my Christian life.

Food for thought

A very dear friend of mine started the ministry IGEM. He is someone who has always been in my life as a 'big brother' and accountability partner in the things of Christ. Over the years, our relationship has grown, and we have continued to stay in touch. We have a lovely relationship guided by the Holy Spirit. The events at this meeting shook me, and reading the testimonies brings it all back. I believe it is crucial that I share how, right before my eyes, I have seen the benefits of obeying nonsense in my lifetime.

I woke up one morning in August 2023 with a heated direction in my spirit, that I had to deliver copies of an "Available Vessel for the Lord's Pleasure" and "Did I Bear Fruits?" to this very good friend of mine mentioned above—two copies of each book, one for him and one for his wife. I knew it had to be done immediately. I rushed quickly to Auntie Kuukua's house and normally I would wait for her to autograph them, but she wasn't home, and I could not wait because I felt I had to obey the instructions immediately. I quickly picked up the books and headed straight to deliver them to my friend, and my part was done.

Fast forward to a few months down the line in 2023. This friend of mine was done reading the books, and he was greatly impacted. He was eager to come to a Meet the Author Series meeting. What happened after that meeting is the beginning of a journey and mentorship between him and Auntie Kuukua, which subsequently led to her speaking at his ministry IGEM.

Why is this so meaningful to me? This is so meaningful to me because I was at that meeting, and I witnessed what the Holy Spirit did that evening. Right before me, I saw how Auntie Kuukua was used mightily by the Holy Spirit that evening.

There were just a handful of people gathered, yet the Holy Spirit ministered so mightily as though there were thousands of people gathered. I learnt two profound things from that meeting: the first was that each individual is equal to thousands of people and can affect millions of lives. Initially, I wondered about the handful of people, yet the Holy Spirit explained that 'I saw a handful of people, but He saw millions of people.' Each individual would affect the lives of many. I have learnt that an individual is called, not because that person is part of a particular group, but because that person has been picked out by God to make an impact.

The second thing I learnt from that meeting still gives me chills even as I recount it now. As I stood at the meeting, I was deeply humbled. Humbled and shaken because I could see the results of the prompt obedience on the day I delivered the books to my friend. What shook my core was what disobeying that instruction could have caused. What if I made an excuse and dismissed the Holy Spirit and assumed that everything was my mind playing games or it was me just speaking to myself? Lord have mercy!! Yet in that meeting, I literally experienced the benefits of Obeying 'Nonsense!' Is there something you're delaying in doing? Is there something that you think doesn't add up or makes no sense in your mind so you will not obey? Is there a person that you're meant to speak to and reach out to? Please remember, that person is equal to millions of people. When I ponder on everything, I am deeply moved by the realisation that what happened at the meeting at IGEM didn't start with my obedience, it started with the obedience of Auntie Kuukua to write the book An Available Vessel for the Lord's Pleasure. What if my friend hadn't given me the book? What if I had also not given the book to my friend… what if, what if, what if ???

My dear friend, let us keep obeying the still small voice when we hear it. Let us not dismiss it as 'Nonsense.'

CHAPTER 17

HEART CLEANSING (2)

In February 2024, I was invited to be the main speaker for a breakfast meeting at the Accra Ridge Church[39]. I was excited and accepted the invitation. As usual, I started praying into the meeting a few days before the date. One evening as I prayed, the Holy Spirit asked me this question, *"What is done at a breakfast meeting?"* I replied that usually at these breakfast meetings you are supposed to share your testimony as the main speaker. Then He said, *'I have told you that you are an available vessel. Anytime you are asked to speak I will tell you what to do, and what to say at the meeting. You only have to avail yourself for me to use'* I said, 'Yes Sir!'

Then He said, *'You are not going to share your testimony, you are going to tell them to cleanse their hearts. That's why I gave you the wisdom to put over forty years of your life in a book. Ask them to get copies of your book, An Available Vessel for the Lord's Pleasure and read, but what I want you to tell them when you mount the stage is that they should cleanse their hearts."*

---

39 *The Accra Ridge Church, an Interdenominational, International, Congregation serviced by Ministers from the Anglican, Methodist and Presbyterian Churches of Ghana. It is located in the residential neighbourhood of Ridge in the capital city of Accra, Ghana.*

I am sure you can imagine this was not an easy task because, this church has congregants who are in their 60s, early 70s, and over 80 years of age. How do I go and tell them to cleanse their hearts? To all intents and purposes, they would be expecting the main speaker to share her testimony.

Once again, I obeyed and when I took the microphone, I told them exactly what the Holy Spirit had said. I told them that my mission there was not to share my testimony because my testimony is in my book, *An Available Vessel for the Lord's Pleasure*, but my mission was to tell them to cleanse their hearts.

As the meeting progressed, the Holy Spirit started ministering to me that each person there was at loggerheads with someone. Either someone was not talking to a parent, siblings were not talking to each other, work colleagues were not talking to each other, and even within the same church, there were departmental fights. The Holy Spirit told me to give them five minutes. He asked them to pick up their phone and reconcile with anyone they had issues with, anybody that they hadn't spoken to, or were not talking to, or hadn't spoken to since the beginning of the year, they should take up their phones and say Happy New Year to the people.

The members reached for their gadgets and started the reconciliation exercise. The Holy Spirit took over the meeting - some of them broke down in tears - there was a lot of weeping. You could tell there was true repentance. The following testimonies are from two people who were present at that meeting. They share how the message impacted them in a timely fashion.

Testimonies

I faced a painful experience of injustice at the hands of two family members. One sold family land illegally, while the other benefited from family land compensation unduly. The hurt and betrayal I felt were overwhelming.

However, as I sought God's guidance and strength, I came to a profound realization: judgment doesn't reside in my own strength but with God. I've learnt not to trust in human justice but to trust in God's divine justice. I've also come to understand the importance of praying for the people that have wronged me, just as Christ taught us to love and pray for our enemies. Even though forgiveness doesn't erase the injustice done to me, it frees my mind and heart from the burden of resentment and bitterness.

Through this experience, I've discovered that forgiveness is not for the ones who wronged me, but for my healing and freedom. As I have forgiven, I am now able to undertake useful endeavours that promote my Christian life and bear fruits for God's kingdom. Fruits of love, compassion, self-control, and sympathy towards all people.

I'm grateful for God's unwavering love and support throughout this journey.

May my testimony encourage others to seek God's strength and grace in their struggles and may we all learn to forgive and love as Christ has loved us.

- *George*

In February 2024, I attended a breakfast meeting, and I was looking forward to hearing Kuukua's testimony. Instead, she shared a word on the importance of having a clean heart. It was a good reminder of how not to take offence.

I thought it was only a good reminder, not knowing that later that day, I would be faced with a challenge which would require me to put into practice what I had been reminded of that morning.

Later that day I engaged with our family head, who ended up saying and behaving in the most unwarranted and unsavoury manner.

What he said justified an equally unsavoury response from me but, just when I was in the throes of being moody and upset, I remembered what had taken place earlier at the meeting. I remembered the message from that morning and I did all I could to push back the temptation of the flesh to retaliate. It was not easy, but as time wore on, I managed to reject the urge to allow offence to take root in my heart.

I'm grateful to the Holy Spirit for being the good Teacher, I thank Him for the timely teaching on offence that morning.

- *Fafa*

Food for thought

I was born into and grew up in the Presbyterian Church. Interestingly, Accra Ridge Church is my childhood church, and that is where my children attend Sunday school.

I was at this breakfast meeting; it was the first of its kind. It was indeed a Holy Spirit-filled breaking of a fast.

The meeting made me realise that the Holy Spirit is doing something with this generation. He is breaking protocols. He's breaking human religious traditions and expectations. He's moving as the Holy Spirit is supposed to move, like a wind and very unpredictable. We don't know where He's coming from or where He's going, Hallelujah!

You may be wondering what I am going on about. First of all, the breakfast turned into a lunch affair. How? Usually the main speaker speaks after breakfast has been served, that is the protocol. However, during the song ministration that followed after the 1st testifier had spoken, Auntie Kuukua felt led to speak after that particular song. She indicated that the song ministration had created an atmosphere such that it would be prudent for her to speak at that time instead of after breakfast had been served.

I was surprised when the organisers agreed. That was the first shocker. I was surprised because Ridge church is noted for sticking to protocols. Yet they agreed and made a change to the program.

The second thing that surprised me was when I saw how the older generation sat through and participated in all the directions given by Auntie Kuukua during the meeting. It was a beautiful experience.

Witnessing this made me ponder on all our religious rules and regulations, and I realised that we indeed limit the Holy Spirit's move in our midst. I believe that sometimes we are too "religious" and stifle the growth of the Holy Spirit in our lives. Maybe we have too many filters to filter the instructions of the Holy Spirit such that we end up not obeying at all!

I acknowledge that being religious serves a purpose, and having a plan serves a purpose. Yet, being in absolute commune with the Holy Spirit serves a greater purpose. The all-knowing Spirit of God that dwells within us indicates where, when, what and how we should go about our day. However, usually, we are so certain we already know our plans (symptoms of religion and religiosity) such that we end up doing what we had already planned and miss out on the blessings derived from obedience to the Holy Spirit.

I was amazed at what happened at the breakfast meeting that morning, how the Holy Spirit broke tradition and took over the service as though it were a revival camp meeting. Everyone expecting to eat breakfast as they listened to a testimony being recounted was greatly off the marker. The Holy Spirit's agenda was to serve a 'clean heart' for breakfast and indeed we were spiritually fed!

But, more importantly, I was amazed at how the older generation who may have been sticklers for traditional orthodox practices and so forth, embraced the ministry and the move of the Holy Spirit that morning. God bless us all, as we unlearn some religious actions and allow the Spirit of God to be the Spirit of God. Amen!

CHAPTER 18

GUARD YOUR HEART

In Chapter 6 of this book, I stated that the Holy Spirit had impressed upon my heart to gather a group of ladies and speak to them on how to guard the heart. This meeting was held on May 1, 2024.

From the time that the instructions were given to me at the beginning of the year, I had studied and prepared on the topic and therefore showed up in all readiness to be used as a vessel for the Lord's pleasure.

The meeting was scheduled to start at 8 am. Interestingly, there was a heavy rainstorm at dawn on that day. I started wondering whether people would show up. God being so good, they did show up, albeit some of them were late. I was there with my keyboardist at 7:45 am. By 8 am, he started playing some worship songs. I decided I would let the worship go on for a while to prepare the atmosphere for the meeting. However, about thirty minutes into the worship, I heard, *'Don't interrupt the music, don't disturb the presence. Don't talk.'*

I wrongly assumed that would go on for only a few minutes. This continued for four solid hours!! The Holy Spirit took over the meeting completely, I didn't have to say a word.

Just about forty-five minutes into the program, self-deliverance started occurring amongst the people gathered there. Some of the people started crying, others fell under the anointing and started coughing and vomiting, whilst others just burst out into laughter and laughed uncontrollably for close to twenty minutes.

To be honest, I was initially scared. That had never happened in any of my meetings before. I was not prepared for most of what happened in that meeting but I believe that in that time, the Holy Spirit cleansed hearts! He removed strongholds! He replaced embittered hearts, He removed iniquities, and He strengthened feeble arms. I am sure He ministered to every single one of the people in the auditorium that morning.

The music never ceased. The praise and worship continued until the end of the meeting after four hours. It was a wonderful time in the presence of the Lord. Indeed, I believe that that day, all the Holy Spirit was looking for was a vessel to avail herself so He would show up and do what pleased Him. I believe the people there needed to see this. They needed to see that the Holy Spirit does what He pleases, and no one can question Him. They needed to see that the Holy Spirit does not only move when there is preaching and or laying on of hands amidst shouting and clapping of hands.

I didn't utter a word, yet the presence of the Holy Spirit was tangible, and I believe it will linger there for weeks and months to come.

I learnt a very good lesson that day. I learnt that when you rely on the Holy Spirit, you can never be prepared enough. He will always do what pleases Him, all you are is just an available vessel. Glory to Jesus!

Testimony

My name is Asempa. I am one of three intercessors who have been praying with Auntie Kuukua since 2015. I was at the May 1 meeting, and I must admit, I have seen Auntie Kuukua minister in meetings, but this one was very different. She was just singing and dancing, yet the Holy Spirit was moving in the room and touching people in diverse ways.

At about 11:50 am I saw her finally sit down quietly. About five minutes later she beckoned to the organist to have the microphone. She then announced that the meeting was over so everyone could go home. She continued and said that she had prepared for the meeting and had many scriptures she thought she was going to use but that when the worship started, the Holy Spirit told her not to interrupt the flow of the meeting and that the Holy Spirit kept repeating that throughout the period we sang and danced.

When I listened to her speak at the end of the meeting, it looked like she was not sure if because she did not preach or teach, the people had not received impartation, because we are used to preaching and teaching and laying of hands at retreats. But, she had nothing to worry about and this is because the intercessors and I remembered something interesting when we left the venue of the meeting.

We remembered that sometime in 2023, at one of the prayer sessions at Auntie Kuukua's house, I got a revelation. In the revelation, I saw that Auntie Kuukua was leading a meeting. She seemed to be standing there and saying nothing, yet I could see many manifestations of the Holy Spirit in the meeting. Some of the people I saw in the revelation were slain under the anointing, others were laughing, others crying etc. That was when it struck us: we had seen this meeting almost a year before it happened in the physical realm.

The Holy Spirit indeed grants us revelations ahead of time. That meeting, indeed, was a Holy Spirit-led meeting and I am so glad I was a part of it. Glory to Jesus.

Food for thought
A ministration without words.
How do I use words to describe a ministration without words? You should have been there is all I can say.

I desire such a deep love relationship with the Holy Spirit such that the tangible force of His presence always continues to rest on me wherever I am! The good news is that this is possible for everyone who believes in Christ

The experience of this meeting brought to mind the lyrics of Don Moen's Hallelujah[40] song specifically the second stanza and chorus, it reads:

Release Your power
To work in us and through us
Till we are changed
To be more like You
Then all the nations will see
Your glory revealed
And worship You.

Hallelujah! Hallelujah! Hallelujah!
To the Lamb
Hallelujah! Hallelujah
By the blood of Christ, we stand
Every tongue every tribe
Every people every land
Giving glory giving honour
Giving praise unto the Lamb of God

---

40 Don Moen is an American singer, pianist, and songwriter, specializing in Christian worship music. He released Hallelujah to the Lamb in 1997 in the Album, 'Let Your Glory Fall'.

Please join me as we declare over our lives!
I will be An Available Vessel for the Lord's Pleasure! Amen
I will be ready to obey with all I have! Amen
I will seek first the Kingdom of God and His righteousness! Amen
I will recognize that the Spirit of the Lord is amongst us and not just behind the pulpit! Amen
I will do the will of God! Amen
I will love as God loves! Amen
I will be led by the Spirit of God! Amen
May the Spirit of the Lord embrace us! Amen

CHAPTER 19

GUARD YOUR HEART AND YOUR TONGUE

My Chapter of the Full Gospel Business Men's Fellowship International, the Crystal Chapter, gave me a slot to speak on May 16, 2024. The topic the Holy Spirit dropped in my spirit was, *'Guard your heart and your tongue.'*

As stated in the previous chapter, I had the opportunity to speak on guarding the heart when I met the ladies on May 1. However, that meeting ended up being more about worship, so I did not speak about any of the things the Holy Spirit had taught me months prior, leading to that particular meeting. Therefore I had several things I knew I could speak about at the Crystal Chapter meeting.

A few days before the meeting, I started asking the Holy Spirit to show me exactly what to talk about as I had many things on my mind, but I also knew that the time slot was just forty-five minutes.

Two days before the meeting, He said I should talk to them about Food. If you may recall, that is one of the items He had drawn my attention to when I was preparing for the May 1 meeting. However, this time, He gave me an interesting angle.

He asked me to look at Psalm 66:18, *'if I regard iniquity in my heart, the Lord will not hear me.'*

When I read that scripture, I became confused because I didn't see the connection with food, so I decided to do research on iniquity and that took me to the seven deadly sins. I don't think I had heard or read anything about that before. One of the seven deadly sins is Gluttony. It was at that point He made the connection and said, *'stay on Gluttony.'*

Are you confused? Don't worry, I was also confused initially.

Let me issue a disclaimer here for Bible scholars and interpreters of the Bible. The Holy Spirit didn't tell me that what I am about to share is the interpretation of the various scriptures. He However used the various scriptures to teach me an invaluable lesson.

He reminded me that as I prepared for the May 1 meeting, He had made a statement *'It is your body, but it is my temple.'*

He drew my attention to 1 Corinthians 3: 16 & 17:

"Do you not know that you are the temple of God and that the Spirit of God dwells in you? If anyone defiles the temple of God, God will destroy him. For the temple of God is holy, which temple you are."

and 1 Corinthians 6:19 & 20:

"Or do you not know that your body is the temple of the Holy Spirit who is in you, whom you have from God, and you are not your own? For you were bought at a price; therefore, glorify God in your body and in your spirit, which is God's."

These scriptures talk about the fact that our body is the temple of God. He further went on to remind me that He had told me that even though our body is His temple, we do not pay attention to what we put in our bodies. We eat anything that comes to mind and at any time of the day without any regard for how that lifestyle impacts the body.

He said that anytime those two scriptures were quoted, they were quoted in reference to sins of the flesh like adultery and fornication, but He wanted me to reflect on what food does to our body, which is His temple. This is where Gluttony comes in i.e. eating and drinking in excess.

He drew my attention to the fact that most of the time, even though we know we are satisfied with the portion of a meal, yet we convince ourselves that if we don't finish the food, it would be wasted so we rather 'dump' the food in the body. No wonder He said we treat His body like a rubbish dump.

My dear friend, according to Psalm 66:18, *'if we regard iniquity in our heart, He will not hear us.'* If Gluttony is iniquity, does that mean that when we are gluttonous and we pray He doesn't hear? That is food for thought.

I must say the meeting was very insightful. As usual He asked me to take the people at the meeting through an exercise.

Each person was to write down one thing he or she would struggle to stop eating if the Lord asked him or her to do so. We had varied interesting answers: Chicken, refined sugar, Coca-Cola, dried coconut etc. etc. I then asked each person to fast on the particular food item for the next two weeks and share their experiences with us the next time we met. I also asked all the people present to endeavour to have their medicals done as soon as possible.

My dear friend, are you gluttonous?

Food for thought (Pun intended)

In January of this year, Auntie Kuukua shared with the Meet the Author team an interesting fast the Holy Spirit had placed her on. She was on a flour fast. Well, that's easy you may say if flour isn't your nemesis. It turned out that most of her foods were flour-based and she hadn't realised it until she was asked to fast on flour i.e. she was not to eat anything made of flour. After sharing her fast details, she asked us to each name the one thing we knew we ate too frequently. We all named our food nemesis, mine was chicken, and another teammate had the same food challenge. Other team members were also hooked unto flour-based foods and another team member who wasn't a foodie admitted that social media was her inescapable joy!

After we identified these, Auntie Kuukua went on to share the remainder of the instructions. We were to go on a month-long fast by not eating anything that had chicken, meat and flour in it, depending on our weakness.

The test was in the discipline of controlling gluttonous desire. On the second day of the fast I had a horrid dream and saw a weird sickly creature that would come alive every time I was served meat and chicken, and instead of me eating the food served it was that creature who would gobble it all up without restraint and control. I then heard that the creature was gluttony.

After that dream, every time I saw chicken and meat, I would get flashbacks and say to myself, 'I'd rather stay away than feed such a horrid creature!' I remember the creature was so skinny, yet it ate ravenously. In this description of it, I learnt why wrongful desires are insatiable and I was enlightened on this; no matter how much you feed a wrongful desire it will always seek more! Feeding a wrongful desire doesn't satisfy it. When it comes to some things, discipline and positive character are what can deal with them.

The first couple of weeks were a bit of a struggle between the flesh and the Spirit. The Holy Spirit, our ever-present guide showed me different equally enjoyable protein forms. By the end of the month, I was certain I was going to be vegan. I felt healthy and different, especially because I had monitored what I ate, and I was certain healthy food had gone into my body.

In Chapter 13's Food for Thought, I shared how I obeyed an instruction to undergo full medicals this year. Here, I would like to share one key thing the medicals revealed and the power of the love of God. The medical exams review indicated that I had high bilirubin levels (in plain language I was jaundiced) and this could lead to liver failure if not treated. I share this because this is one of the silent killers if not detected early. Its symptoms can be easily ignored as 'stress and tiredness.' A dietary change and a healthy lifestyle were prescribed immediately. I can now pray and mention by name any ailment that wants to mess with me, and I can live intentionally treating the body as the temple it is.

At the Crystal Chapter meeting, Jainie the Chapter president shared an interesting insight. He shared the importance of the human body to the work of God on earth. God needs to use the human body on earth to work in this space because that is the regulation He God put in place to govern the operation of the earth. That is why Christ came to earth in Human form and didn't just operate as a Spirit in a vacuum. If we continue to neglect the temple of God which is our body, we limit the work of God in our lives and the lives of others. We cannot continue to die from preventable ailments that require a lifestyle change to conquer. We cannot preach to God and neglect His temple.

May God help us all!

PART THREE

CHAPTER PRELUDE

In the third part of this book, I share testimonies from a few readers of my first book *An Available Vessel for the Lords Pleasure*. These testimonies were shared at the Meet the Author Series (MTA) meetings between October 2023 and April 2024.

MTA is a meeting the Holy Spirit impressed on me to start in September 2023. It is a program designed to raise 'Available Vessels.' It is made up of a series of events where readers get to meet and interact with me on any of my books, *An Available Vessel for the Lord's Pleasure, Did I Bear Fruits? and The Benefits of Obeying 'Nonsense.'*

These events are intimate gatherings focused on discussing the testimonies in the books, the role of the Holy Spirit in my life and His impact on the readers. This is a quarterly meeting.

The mission of these meetings is to ensure that everybody who reads *An Available Vessel for the Lord's Pleasure* bears spiritual fruits. Every meeting is unique as it hosts a different set of guests each time, and with every group comes beautiful testimonies and revelations. In two hours, we generally talk about the goodness of the Holy Spirit and how to grow in Him.

We have discussed profound topics over the months. These topics have touched on healing, liberty, giving, overcoming sexual sins, deliverance and forgiveness. At a few notable meetings, the themes of forgiveness and the cleansing of the heart were discussed. Incidentally, most of the guests shared their challenges with unforgiveness and how the Holy Spirit had used my book *An Available Vessel for the Lord's Pleasure* to heal or start the healing process of their hearts. These are a few testimonies that were shared at the meetings. However, to give context to the testimonies from the meetings, I have copied the stories in *An Available Vessel for the Lord's Pleasure* that formed the basis of their testimonies: *'Do Penance'*, *'He Is Not Talking to Someone'* and *'Forgiveness Saves the Soul.'*

CHAPTER 20

DO PENANCE

I had a very bad relationship with my mother. Looking back, I don't recall how it started, but as long as I can remember until about fifteen years ago, my mom and I had a turbulent relationship that would be the source of many meetings between myself and my grandparents, my uncles, and aunties, at various stages when I was growing up. There were so many meetings, even with pastors of the church she was attending at that time, at a point, I felt like I was the devil incarnate.

Such was the relationship that one day as she was speaking to me and attempted to hit me, I blocked her hand and landed a hefty slap on her face. When I was getting married to my childhood sweetheart at age twenty-two, she was not in agreement. In a heated argument, she said, *"You will go and come back and recognise that I am your mother."* I did go, and returned three years into the marriage, according to her words.

On another occasion, my mum was returning home from an outing. When I heard the car come in, I turned to my little sister and said, *"There comes the witch"* and walked away into my room. I simply could not stand the sight of her. When you mentioned her name to me, I would get goosebumps out of sheer irritation. When I finished sixth form, I moved from Cape Coast[41] to live with her in Accra. I lived with her through my National Service until I finished law school.

During this period, between 1995 and 2002, we would argue about one thing or the other. We never seemed to agree on anything. Even though we lived in the same house, the relationship had deteriorated so much that she would leave notes for me on the kitchen table when going out and I would do likewise when I was going out. My joy knew no bounds when I got the opportunity to go to Koforidua for my second National Service. For me, that was freedom at last. Now I could live by myself on my terms without her breathing down my neck, I thought.

Interestingly, it seemed as though the relationship started turning out for the better when we started living apart. To the best of my recollection, what brought a dramatic change in our relationship was the birth of my niece, Kayla. I maintained and still do, that Kayla is my Angel on assignment. My sister had Kayla in the U.K. When she came back, she lived with my mother. I still can't put my finger on exactly what it was, but I simply fell in love with that baby girl. I could never have enough of her. By the time she was five years old, I could be seen everywhere I went with her. She kept telling my mother to bring her to my house, and so my mum would call me and say, *"Your daughter wants to*

---

41 *Cape Coast is the capital of the Central Region, in southern Ghana. It's known for its role in the transatlantic slave trade. It is the site for the Cape Coast Castle, which is a large, whitewashed fort built by the Swedish in the 17th century.*

talk to you." I would also call and tell her to give the phone to Kayla so I could talk with her. That was what improved the communication gap that had existed between us for years.

My niece was born around the time that I had been introduced to prayer at the Prayer Cafe. A few years later, I got acquainted with Reverend Paul Adu as well.

By this time, a lot of prayers and prophecies were coming up about my marriage. There seemed to be quite a bit of warfare needed if I was to break through to get married.

It was during this period that one night, as I knelt by my bed praying in the Spirit, I heard it loud and clear, *"You have to do penance."* Now I was sure I knew the meaning of the word penance, but I still googled it. Google gave me, *"Punishment inflicted on oneself as an outward expression of repentance for wrongdoing."* The second meaning I got was, *"a sacrament in which a member of the Church confesses sins to a priest and is given absolution."*

After reading it, I said to the Holy Spirit: *"Why do you say so? What have I done that I need to do penance for?"* His response was, *"Honour thy father and mother, so that it may be well with you."* And He continued, *"You have been praying for a life partner for a few years now and before I release him unto you, you need to make penance for all the wrongdoing towards your mother."* Then He added, *"Buy a brand-new car for your mother."*

The Holy Spirit has never been wrong, my dear friend. At about this time, the vehicle my mom was using was very old and had started giving her problems. The very next morning

I went to the bank to redeem treasury bills I had invested in. When the money was ready, I cashed it and went to Rana Motors[42] to buy her the latest Four-wheel Kia on the market that year.

Three weeks after I sent her the vehicle, a gentleman who had been my friend for years proposed to marry me. That was the first marriage proposal since I ended my first engagement in 1999.

Now I don't know about you, but I do see a connection between the penance and the marriage proposal. What did I learn from this incident? That all scripture is true? The Bible says, *"Honour your father and mother so it shall be well with you."* I had dishonoured my mother for years and the Lord out of His mercy and abundant compassion, through the power of the Holy Spirit helped me to right the wrong so I would enjoy the spiritual blessings associated with the first command in the Bible, with a promise; *"So it shall be well with you."* Amen.

---

42 Rana Motors: KIA authorized dealership in Ghana.

CHAPTER 21

HE IS NOT TALKING TO SOMEONE

At one of the Morning Glory meetings held at Action Chapel, a man of God was leading us in repeating some declarations.

Then, I heard a man just behind me shout, "*God, why is it not happening for me?!*" I turned to look at him and the Holy Spirit whispered, *"Because he is not talking to someone."* I didn't say anything to him. A few more weeks passed by before I saw him at the meetings again. The Holy Spirit nudged me to go and talk to him and tell him what He told me the other day.

This gentleman was not someone I knew. I would occasionally see him at *Morning Glory*. The nature of this prayer meeting did not allow room for people to be chatty. It is a place where people come to pray and seek the face of the Lord. However, I proceeded to engage this gentleman in a conversation. I asked if he remembered the incident the last time he had come to pray and he said *"Yes."* I told him that when he queried *"God, why is it not happening for me?"* the Holy Spirit told me that it was because he was not talking to someone.

I told him that the Holy Spirit had said that what happened with the person was not his fault and that he was right. However, the devil wanted to gain access to his life. The foothold that had given the devil access to his life was unforgiveness and the hurt he was still holding against that person. The Holy Spirit was instructing him to give the person a call and leave it at that.

He looked at me quietly, said *thank you* and walked away. The next time I lay eyes on him, he was lying prostrate at the altar weeping and praying. I became very concerned and asked myself, *"Eii what have I just done?"* The next morning, he came up to me and said, *"My sister, thank you and God bless you so much for what you told me yesterday."* Then he added, *"*You are right. That incident was Twenty-eight years ago.*"* I was shocked. *Twenty-eight years?* I couldn't believe it.

This is when the Holy Spirit began to minister to me. He told me about how the devil succeeds in blocking our blessings. He told me how unforgiveness is a powerful tool the devil uses to ensnare us. This, the Holy Spirit said, is a big challenge for Christians. He said that we are good at fasting and attending all manner of prayer meetings, but we hold grudges and unforgiveness in our hearts, and when that happens, all the efforts we put into praying and fasting are to no avail.

I was amazed at this revelation but more so about the leadings of the Holy Spirit. Things were not going well for him because he had not talked to someone for twenty-eight years. There is no way I could have guessed this.

My dear friend, would you please pause at this point and examine yourself:

i. Is there someone who has hurt you so badly that you have stopped talking to him or her?
ii. Are you holding unforgiveness in your heart?
iii. Is life going the way you want it to or are you frustrated with what is happening?
iv. Could it be that you are not having your prayers answered because you are holding a grudge against someone?

Please empty yourself. The Bible says in *1 John 8-9*, *"If we say we have no sin, we deceive ourselves and the truth is not in us. But if we confess our sins, He is faithful and just to cleanse us from all unrighteousness."* Let the Holy Spirit help you start over. Let him position you to experience unfailing love and abundant blessings. Unforgiveness kills us and robs us of the joy of the Lord and good health.

May the holy spirit give us understanding and shine His light on every part of our lives that is in darkness so that we may experience the power of Christ. Amen!

CHAPTER 22

FORGIVENESS SAVES THE SOUL

My name is Felicia Frimpong and I have known Auntie Kuukua for about three years. I am a qualified Montessori school teacher with certification from the Montessori Institute in Weija[43], a suburb of Accra, Ghana. After my training, I was offered a role to be a home teacher for two children. These two children happened to be the sons of Kuukua Maurice Ankrah, and that's how we met.

Some years into working with Auntie Kuukua, I was also making arrangements for my wedding. I got pregnant during our courtship, and everything began to take a nosedive. I was having issues with my mother-in-law, who was against the marriage on the grounds of the pregnancy. I was also expecting that my boyfriend would fight back on my behalf. The pains and disappointments from the events within this period made me hate and despise him. I had gradually gathered offence in my heart against him. I proceeded to block him from all communication channels.

---

43 *Weija is a small town and is the capital of Ga South Municipal District, a district in the Greater Accra Region of Ghana.*

I had become depressed, sad, and looked miserable and heavily pregnant. During this period my already shaky Christian life dwindled the more.

As a Sunday school teacher, I had ceased to attend church, let alone go and teach the children. I had stopped praying. I craved someone to nag with, and someone who would sympathise with me.

During this same period, I spoke to Auntie Kuukua about what I was going through. She comforted me and advised me. Then she gave me a book on forgiveness. I didn't realise the connection between the subject and what I was going through, but the Holy Spirit through that book ministered to me more than I thought. From the book, I learnt about the story of a five-year-old boy who died because his mother was careless and distracted by so many things, and so could not pray for him when he was developing as a baby in her womb. The boy died of kidney failure. It was obvious that the boy would have lived if the mother had made time to pray for him. When I read that story, I sensed in my spirit that the Holy Spirit was giving me a message. The message was, *"Felicia, use this time to pray for your baby so that it will develop well. Do not spend it to justify your hatred or pain."*

Upon hearing that, I decided to concentrate on the baby that was developing in my womb. Instead of complaining and murmuring, I was praying that the baby's organs would develop well. I was also praying for a safe delivery.

I was beginning to develop the leading to forgiveness. I had not fully understood what it meant to be led by the Holy Spirit and the role of speaking in tongues. Auntie

Kuukua started taking me to programmes at Action Chapel International. She started taking me to Dominion Hour prayer meetings. She also took me to Impact[44] 2019. Prophet Akwasi Agyeman Prempeh[45] was ministering on that day we went. That service was memorable because it was on that day that I received the baptism of the Holy Spirit with the evidence of speaking in tongues. My life took a positive turn after that experience.

One day, I had a prompting in my spirit to call my baby's father. I hesitated at first, but eventually, I picked up my phone and called him. I spoke to him nicely for the first time without even realising. He told me how things had taken a downward turn after he rescinded his promise to marry me. He had become addicted to alcohol. He told me that he was surprised that I called him. I began to heed the prompting of the Holy Spirit. We prayed and I told him I had forgiven him.

That phone call was proof of what the Holy Spirit had been doing in my life since Auntie Kuukua gave me the book. I continued to go for my antenatal care and had an easy delivery after forty weeks of pregnancy by the grace of God. There were no complications, there were no problems. Everything went on well by the grace of God.

Auntie Kuukua is a woman of prayer. I am following in her steps. I believe the Holy Spirit will help me develop my prayer life as he has helped Auntie Kuukua to develop hers.

---

44 *Impact is an annual convention of Action Chapel International, featuring a host of speakers from across the globe.*
45 *Prophet Akwasi Agyemang Prempeh is the general overseer of the Ultimate Charismatic Centre, Accra Ghana.*

I am a single mum. I couldn't marry the man I wanted to marry but I believe all things have worked together for my good and I give glory to God. My baby is doing well by the grace of God.

When Samuel and John started formal school, I became jobless. But in August of the same year, Action Chapel started the school: Dominion Christian Academy[46]. Auntie Kuukua spoke to the Head of the school, who was recruiting fresh teachers at that time. I was interviewed and given a job a few days later. I am currently a Pre-KG teacher at Dominion Christian Academy.

To anyone reading this testimony, I would like to say this. I didn't know God would use Auntie Kuukua to impact my spiritual life to the level where I could depend on the Holy Spirit to forgive someone who disappointed me and be able to pray by myself. All glory to Jesus.

---

46 *Dominion Christin Academy is a Cambridge and American International School in Accra Ghana.*

TESTIMONIES FROM 'MEET THE AUTHOR SERIES' MEETINGS

CHAPTER 23

LET IT GO

I received a copy of *An Available Vessel for the Lord's Pleasure* from a friend, Bob. Every testimony was a blessing. After reading the book I got invited to the Meet the Author Series held by the author Kuukua Maurice Ankrah. At this meeting, I got to meet and fellowship with the author. The meeting was amazing, it felt like a great Christian avenue to freely talk about the Holy Spirit and His role in our lives. It also felt like a safe support community, I left the meeting that day feeling very full and satisfied with the word. At this meeting, I shared how the Holy Spirit through the testimony on forgiveness in the book *An Available Vessel for the Lord's Pleasure* released me and saved me from hurt and unforgiveness I had been holding onto for years.

I had been holding on to the thoughts of hurt from my daughter's father over the years and I even had kept our chat messages hoping to defend myself with them when the time came. One evening, the thoughts of unforgiveness came so strongly. When I woke up the next day I noticed that my WhatsApp was backing up. This was nothing unusual because it usually happened. Each time I would have all the messages restored after the backup process. However, on this particular day, to my utmost shock, I lost all my WhatsApp messages. Particularly the ones I had been keeping as a defence mechanism against my daughters' father.

Before I could even brood over it…the Holy Spirit told me, *"I just helped you. Let it go."* He taught me to forgive him and let anything I held against him go.

Anita, Media Programs Specialist, testifier from an MTA meeting.

CHAPTER 24

"KEEP A CLEAN HEART, I WILL DO THE REST"

My name is Comfort and I work in the protocol department at Action Chapel International. I have served as an usher for several years. Usually, I was the one who would usher Auntie Kuukua and her husband to their seats. They always sat directly behind me. Although we never spoke, I had noticed how easy-going she and her husband were.

In September 2023 the strangest thing happened. Auntie Kuukua randomly approached me and gave me a word which was an answer to a prayer I had just prayed on the altar. She later on gave me a copy of her book *An Available Vessel for the Lords Pleasure*. When that incident happened, I was dumbfounded and in shock for several reasons, the main one being that God had remembered me and answered my prayer through His Vessel.

I had struggled with self-doubt and insecurities for years. Unfortunately, as an usher sometimes some people tend to look down on you and treat you with disdain. Later when

I got home and started reading the book I was even more surprised. The truth is that I did not know the pedigree of Auntie Kuukua and her husband. I accorded them respect because I love to do my job as an usher with joy and diligence. I have encountered some pretty uptight people in my duty, so to find out that Auntie Kuukua was such a spiritual vessel and yet remained humble and had responded to me with respect every Sunday for years was awesome!

The book was a blessing! My spiritual life leapt, my confidence has shot up, my insecurities are no more, and I am walking in awareness that I can be humble and yet confident! I am currently the protocol head of the MTA meetings.

One major transformation that took place in me when I read *An Available Vessel for the Lord's Pleasure* was about my heart. After the burial of my brother a few years ago, I was struck with an illness. Although I looked well on the outside, I was slowly fading away on the inside. I could feel my spirit leave my body and I felt hollow.

One day, I approached one of our Bishops at church to pray with me. He was surprised and even remarked that I didn't look sick, yet I insisted he prayed for me because I knew what I was going through was not normal or physical. I couldn't eat, I was losing weight, and I was a shell of my former self.

After I read the book *An Available Vessel for the Lord's Pleasure*, I had a dream. In the dream, I believe I saw the Lord in a vivid vision. He simply said to me that all I had do was keep a clean heart and He would handle the rest. I woke up revitalized with divine strength, and that was the end of my ailments! I am working on guarding my heart knowing that God handles all that concern me! Hallelujah!

- Comfort, Protocol Head, MTA.
Testifier from an MTA meeting.

CHAPTER 25

CANTANKEROUS? NEVER AGAIN!

My name is Naji. I have known Auntie Kuukua for almost two decades. I am practically a member of her family. Our relationship started with me being her beauty therapist but the relationship has evolved. She has been one of the greatest support systems in my life and family.

I am a practising Muslim, and in relating with Auntie Kuukua I have learnt so much. I have learnt how to listen, how to obey, and how to forgive and be more tolerant. I have read *An Available Vessel for the Lord's Pleasure* and I have my testimony in her second book *Did I Bear Fruits?*, Scene 14. Over the years I have found a confidant in Auntie Kuukua, usually she laughs at me after I recount my problems and she says, *"Your problems are self inflicted."*

Before I met Auntie Kuukua, I was very cantankerous. I could hold onto grudges for a long time. I was always fighting with my husband, and I wouldn't talk to him for days. Usually, Auntie Kuukua would lambast me about it.

I was also always complaining about my parents. I found it

difficult to send money to my father. I would always argue with my mother. One day, Auntie Kuukua said to me, *"Learn to mind your business."* It seemed like a simple instruction, but when I started 'minding my business,' I noticed that I was changing. I am not sure what exactly happened, but I believe simply being around Auntie Kuukua has had a positive impact on my life. I have known her for years, and I have seen how she has handled people who have betrayed her trust and people who have hurt her badly. Most of the time, I am angry when I see that she has forgiven the people and they have started coming around her as if nothing had happened.

It has taken me years, but I believe I have become a much better person. I no longer hold grudges for a long time. Yes, I know, I am still a work in progress. The relationship between my husband and I is much better. I can also say that I have a better relationship with my parents. Generally, I believe she has rubbed off on me a lot. I didn't realize that holding grudges even harmed our health.

If I could do it, trust me, you can also do it. Just take the first step, and the rest will follow.

- Naji, Beauty Therapist, testifier from an MTA meeting.

CHAPTER 26

THE JOURNEY TO TRULY LOVING MY MOTHER

I walked into a shop in Kanda[47] and saw the book *An Available Vessel for the Lord's Pleasure*. I got it immediately because I love reading anything and everything about the Holy Spirit. After reading the book I reached out to the author to share how the book had impacted me deeply. She in turn invited me to join in one of the Meet the Author Series meetings, I was blessed!

One of the profound experiences I had with the book was when I read Chapter 6, *'Do Penance,'* where she shares her journey with her mum. When I got to that story I wept bitterly. It felt as though I was reading my own story. I had been at loggerheads with my mother for years, I always felt that she was not spiritual enough. She is Ga[48] and likes to participate in most Ga traditional rituals, and I despised

---

47 *Kanda Estate is a locality in the Accra Metropolitan District, Greater Accra Region.*
48 *The Ga people belong to the larger Ga-Damgbe group of Kwa-speaking people who inhabit the Greater Accra region of Ghana.*

that. When I read the book, the Holy Spirit convicted me. I wept. I called my mother and went to see her; I apologized to her and bought a piece of cloth and other gifts for her. She accepted my apology, and we are now on good terms.

When I read the book, I realized that I had been practising self-righteousness. I thought that I was more spiritual than my mother, and I had dishonoured her for many years because of that.

My life has been full of ups and downs. From the book, I believe that some of my problems could stem from the kind of relationship I had with my mother. Indeed, it is true that for lack of knowledge, we perish. I believe that in the coming months and years, my life will turn for the better and I will share a testimony to the Glory of God. Amen

- Miriam, testifier from an MTA meeting.

Food for Thought
One of the best ways to spend a Saturday morning is to be at the Meet the Author Series meeting. It is a fantastic two hour period from 10:00 am to 12:00 noon, just sharing testimonies and chatting about the Holy Spirit. It is awesome. As I type this, I have a huge grin on my face as I recall the moments of joy, tears, elation, and the many moving testimonies that have instantly impacted people. One of the first things the Holy Spirit did at the onset of the MTA Series was to caution us (the team members) that it was a place for learning and unlearning. Since then, every single meeting has been phenomenal, because we approach it as

the blessed opportunity it is and not just an exercise to make sure all things are in place for others to be blessed.

Every single meeting is unique, the guests do not return the following week, so in essence every week we have a new set of guests and testimonies. How exciting! At each meeting, we get to experience a whole new dimension of who the person of the Holy Spirit is. He gives us a whole new taste of Himself, a whole new flavour of Himself, and it is exhilarating. I could go on and on and on about how it is a blessing to be at these meetings. I hope we get to see you at one of the meetings when you are done reading this book. Just clear up a Saturday and spend it with other believers chatting about the Holy Spirit for two hours.

The scripture that comes alive whenever there's an MTA meeting is Revelation 12:11, "And they overcame him by the blood of the Lamb and by the word of their testimony, and they did not love their lives to the death." Right in front of our eyes, without a "pulpit" and all the pomp and ceremony that comes with a regular church service, in the simplicity of a small intimate gathering of not more than twenty guests per meeting, seated in a horseshoe manner, the Holy Spirit honours the gathering and glorifies Himself. I hope to see you soon at an MTA meeting armed with testimonies of the Faithfulness of the Lord!

CONCLUSION

My dear reader, I believe you have enjoyed each testimony in this book. What do you say? Could you see yourself in any of us in the book? Releasing people who have offended us from account in our hearts is no easy thing to do, don't get me wrong. However, it is the right thing to do as a child of God.

One of the ways I have managed to keep my heart clean is to declare that no human being is going to make me miss heaven. *Does that help?* Yes, it does.

As you close this book, finally, I pray for you. I pray that the Holy Spirit Himself, who is our Helper, will help you guard your heart. I pray, that NO human being will have so much power over you such that you lose your soul.

May the Lord bless you and keep you all the days of your life. Amen.

BIOGRAPHY OF VICTORIA TWUM-GYAMRAH

Victoria Twum-Gyamrah is a Heritage scientist with a special interest in Coastal Heritage. She is a trained Archaeologist and teaches the discipline at the University of Ghana, Department of Archaeology and Heritage Studies.

Victoria is also a theatre performing artist with Roverman Productions- the leading theatre production house in Ghana, and an Art and Cultural heritage enthusiast.

As a Presbyterian, she has fellowships with the Bethany Presbyterian church in Teshie, and the Accra Ridge Church. She is married to Dr. David Twum-Gyamrah and they have a lovely family.

ALSO BY THE AUTHOR

FOREWORD BY JAINIE AGOVI JAINIE
THE BENEFITS OF
OBEYING
"NONSENSE"
KUUKUA MAURICE ANKRAH
THE BENEFITS OF OBEYING "NONSENSE"
"The Benefits of Obeying 'Nonsense'" is a book for every follower of Jesus Christ who believes that He sent the Holy Spirit, our Helper, to help us on Earth. The author, Kuukua Maurice Ankrah shares various testimonies that demonstrate the importance of listening to and obeying instructions from the Holy Spirit, especially when the instructions don't make sense.
The testimonies that are shared in the book will increase your faith, assure you of the presence of the Holy Spirit in your life (if you have accepted the Lord Jesus as your Personal Saviour), and encourage you to develop a more intimate relationship with Him. You will no longer doubt that the Holy Spirit has been speaking with, through and to you when you thought whatever you kept hearing was 'nonsense.'
May the Holy Spirit brood over you and make you more attentive to Him as you delve into the testimonies in the book.
ABOUT THE AUTHOR
Kuukua Maurice ANKRAH is the author of "An Available Vessel for the Lord's Pleasure" and "Did I Bear Fruits?" She is a Lawyer by profession and a Notary Public of the Republic of Ghana.
She is married to Dr. Emmanuel Maurice ANKRAH a medical doctor and a lawyer by profession. She has four children of whom two boys are her biological children.
She fellowships at the Prayer Cathedral, Action Chapel International, in Accra. She is also a Member of the Airport City Chapter of the Full Gospel Businessmen's Fellowship.
Kuukua is the Managing Partner of KuukuaA Legal Consulting, a legal firm in Accra, Ghana. She started her legal profession at the Attorney General's Department as an Assistant State Attorney. She later joined a private legal firm: LithurBrew & Company where she gained extensive experience in litigation and private practice. She subsequently went back into Public Service when she joined the Ghana Immigration Service and Petroleum Commission between 2006 and 2014. As an entrepreneur, she founded Dudu N J Play Den, an inflatable business in 2017 and LSG Company Ltd, an emergency preparedness training company in 2018.
In January 2023, Kuukua coordinated and birthed 'The Choir on Wheels,' which is a five-member choir made up of an organist and four choristers. The Choir visits the homes of senior citizens and ministers to them through hymns.
ISBN: 978-9988-3-6786-2
9789988367862
"NONSENSE" KUUKUA MAURICE ANKRAH

NOTES

NOTES

NOTES